UNDERSTANDING

GRAHAM GREENE

Understanding Contemporary
British Literature

Matthew J. Bruccoli, *Editor*

Understanding Graham Greene
by R. H. Miller

Understanding Doris Lessing
by Jean Pickering

UNDERSTANDING
Graham
GREENE

by R. H. MILLER

UNIVERSITY OF SOUTH CAROLINA PRESS

To

Diane Partee Miller

with love

Copyright © University of South Carolina 1990

Published in Columbia, South Carolina, by the
University of South Carolina Press

Manufactured in the United States of America

Library of Congress Cataloging-in-Publication Data

Miller, R. H. (Robert Henry), 1938–
    Understanding Graham Greene / by R. H. Miller.
    p.   cm. — (Understanding contemporary British literature)
    Includes bibliographical references.
    ISBN 0–87249–704–6
    1. Greene, Graham, 1904–   —Criticism and interpretation.
  I. Title. II. Series.
   PR6013.R44Z655   1990
823'.912—dc20   90–32677
                                                                 CIP

CONTENTS

237371

EDITOR'S PREFACE

Understanding Contemporary British Literature has been planned as a series of guides or companions for students as well as good nonacademic readers. The editor and publisher perceive a need for these volumes because much of the influential contemporary literature makes special demands. Uninitiated readers encounter difficulty in approaching works that depart from the traditional forms and techniques of prose and poetry. Literature relies on conventions, but the conventions keep evolving; new writers form their own conventions— which in time may become familiar. Put simply, *UCBL* provides instruction in how to read certain contemporary writers—identifying and explicating their material, themes, use of language, point of view, structures, symbolism, and responses to experience.

The word *understanding* in the series title was deliberately chosen. Many willing readers lack an adequate understanding of how contemporary literature works; that is, what the author is attempting to express and the means by which it is conveyed. Although the criticism and analysis in the series have been aimed at a level of general accessibility, these introductory volumes are meant to be applied in conjunction with the works they cover. Thus they do not provide a substitute for the works and authors they introduce, but rather prepare the reader for more profitable literary experiences.

M. J. B.

ACKNOWLEDGMENTS

This study owes a great deal to libraries with extensive collections of Greene's works and papers. I am especially in the debt of the Humanities Research Center, University of Texas, Austin, for their many kindnesses. I also thank the Lilly Library of Indiana University for their assistance. To the Ekstrom Library of the University of Louisville I am especially grateful for continued support of the Graham Greene collection and for providing me with this fine resource. In addition, I wish to thank the British Library for various kinds of assistance.

For a project completion grant that funded much of my travel and work in the final stages I wish to thank President Donald C. Swain and the University of Louisville.

For various kinds of support and encouragement I shall always be in the debt of my colleagues in the Department of English, University of Louisville.

I wish particularly to thank my colleague E. R. Hagemann for his helpful discussions of Greene's work.

UNDERSTANDING

GRAHAM GREENE

CHAPTER ONE

Vista

To understand Graham Greene's novels, plays, and stories one can best consider them as fictions in which two worlds are constantly either resonating or colliding with each other at various points in the narrative flow. One world is outer; it is the geographical place. The other is inner; it is the human heart. What grips Greene's readers in this manifold and complex series of conflicts and resonances is their concern for both worlds, for the fate of a society or a culture on the one hand, and for human beings on the other. Greene is a vigorous observer; he writes from a highly developed moral perspective and invests his narratives with a deep moral concern, most so when in the novel or story there seems no basis for any kind of moral meaning in life. Even the most nihilistic of his visions arise from an anguished cry against the lack of a moral center in the world he critiques.

Some critics note Greene's romantic view of human nature, his insight into the heart of the child, the continual clash in his stories between the corruptions of adulthood and the innocence of childhood, in stories like "The Basement Room" and "I Spy." There is often a Wordsworthian sensibility present in his work. To better understand how Greene came to develop such a vision one needs to look into his life and career, particularly those early years he describes so clearly and dispassionately in his autobiography, *A Sort of Life* (1971).

Life and Career

Greene was born into a comfortable middle-class family on 2 October 1904, in a village that threatens soon to become an outlying suburb northwest of London called Berkhamsted, in Hertfordshire. His parents, both Greenes and first cousins, provided him with the comforts of a large family of three brothers and two sisters, of which he was the fourth born, with servants, with a gracious house and several Greene cousins and other relatives nearby. His father was soon to become headmaster of Berkhamsted School, an event that was to provide Greene with many of the themes of childhood he explored in later years in his writing. The burden of being the son of the headmaster weighed heavily on him, as he describes in many poignant episodes in *A Sort of Life.* The conflicts caused several suicide attempts, culminating finally in his being sent at age fifteen to London for six months of treatment under the psychoanalyst Kenneth Richmond, a remarkably pioneering decision for his parents to make, considering that psychoanalysis was still a relatively new form of therapy.[1] The process must have been influential in assisting Greene to develop his uncanny skill at exploring the interiors of his characters, their motivations and dreams. Greene is obsessed with the subject of dreams, his own and those of his characters.

After completing his public school training Greene was sent up to Oxford in 1922, to Balliol College, where he studied modern history and passed what he describes as a debt-ridden, drunken, desultory existence. He took his BA in 1925 and began a career in journalism, first with the *Nottingham Journal* for six months and then as subeditor with the *Times* of London, where he stayed until 1930. His various efforts at getting published were largely ineffectual until his third novel (his first two remain unpublished), *The Man Within* (1929), which was taken on by William Heinemann Ltd. and proved a success with both readers and critics, so much so as to cause him to quit his job with the *Times* and take handsome but enslaving advances from his publishers, which kept him well in their debt until the publication of *The Heart of the Matter* in 1948.

Greene's other early novels were not so successful. Two were outright failures (*The Name of Action*, 1930, and *Rumour at Nightfall*, 1931); three were modest critical successes but not so financially (*It's a Battlefield*, 1934, *England Made Me*, 1935, and *Brighton Rock*, 1938). Three others proved slightly more so financially; these belonged to a new genre, which Greene called "entertainments" to distinguish them from his more serious "novels," the entertainments being more melodramatic, more focused on action, discovery, on the successful outcome, and less on character. These were the highly successful *Stamboul Train* (1932, American Title *Orient Express*), *A Gun for Sale* (1936, American title *This Gun for Hire*), and *The Confidential Agent* (1939).

During this early period Greene experienced two important changes: his conversion to Roman Catholicism and his marriage. The two events were linked by the fact that his future wife, Vivien Dayrell-Browning, was Catholic, and her sophisticated knowledge of her faith prodded Greene on his own road toward conversion. He took instructions from Father Trollope at the cathedral in Nottingham and was accepted into the Church in 1926. In the next year he married Vivien, and from that marriage he has a daughter, Lucy Caroline, and a son, Francis. By the close of 1939, however, the marriage had begun to come apart, and after the war Graham and Vivien separated permanently, never to divorce. For much of his life Greene has been a wanderer, turning to friendships of longer or shorter duration.

The publication and reception of *Brighton Rock* in 1938 pointed the way toward several powerful novels to come and toward Greene's strengthening grip on stories that bring issues of faith and politics to bear on each other. *Brighton Rock* was only the beginning, to be followed in 1940 by *The Power and the Glory*, in 1948 by *The Heart of the Matter*, and in 1951 by *The End of the Affair*. Greene's early reviewers and critics, and many of his reading public, became preoccupied with his new Catholic concerns, to the neglect of many other notable advances in his art. Greene himself has said he wishes to be thought of as a novelist who happens to be a Catholic, not as a Catholic novelist. In many ways the theological and doctrinal preoccupations of that generation have done him a disservice.[2]

At the outbreak of World War II Greene was doing military duty as an air-raid warden when, through the influence of his sister Elisabeth, he found a post with MI6, the counterintelligence arm of the Secret Service. He was first sent to Sierra Leone, and was from 1941 to 1943 "our man in Freetown." In 1943 and 1944 he served in London in the Iberian section under the notorious Kim Philby, to whom he continued to be a friend and staunch defender after Philby's defection in 1963 until his death in 1988. Greene's career in intelligence came to an end in 1944, but his fascination with it has found voice in several novels, most notably *The Ministry of Fear* (1943), *The Third Man* (1950), *The Quiet American* (1955), *Our Man in Havana* (1958), and *The Human Factor* (1978).

Greene's career from the 1950s to 1968 consisted of continued production of novels and short stories, plays, children's books, essays, two remarkable film scripts

UNDERSTANDING GRAHAM GREENE

(*The Third Man* and *The Fallen Idol*); of journeys to several trouble spots: Malaya, Kenya, Indochina, Haiti, Cuba, the Congo; and reportage done for *Life, Paris-Match,* the *Sunday Times, Le Figaro,* and the *Sunday Telegraph;* and of a soberer but no less distinguished career as a director of the publishing firm of the Bodley Head. His retirement from the business side of publishing came in 1968, but his writing career continues. He lives in a small apartment in Antibes, on the French Riviera, where he writes daily.

Overview of the Writings

Perhaps the most useful way to understand the distinctive qualities of Greene's fiction is to view it in terms of the writers who served as models for its development. Its sense of place, its stress on exotic places or on the strangeness of the familiar world of Greene's England, draw on the writings of Joseph Conrad. Its sense of plot, its emphasis on action, draw on writers from Greene's youthful reading—Robert Louis Stevenson, Stanley Weyman, John Buchan, G. E. Henty, and most importantly H. Rider Haggard—and, to a lesser extent, the American cinema.[3] (Greene was one of the most important early reviewers of films for the *Spectator* during the 1930s and 40s.) Its sense of character development, of the structure of narrative, arises from the influ-

VISTA

ence of Henry James and Charles Dickens, from whom
Greene learned the art of dramatizing inner conflicts,
the conflicts of the heart.

A look at these three discrete aspects as they develop in Greene's fiction and culminate in major themes
in the major novels can tell one a great deal. First, for
setting: In the early novels Greene focused on England,
on places like the West Country in *The Man Within*; London and Nottingham in *It's a Battlefield, A Gun for Sale,*
and *The Confidential Agent*; Brighton in *Brighton Rock*. It
is only in the two failed early novels, *The Name of Action*
and *Rumour at Nightfall,* and in the successful *Stamboul
Train* that Greene ventured beyond England, and in
those novels the settings tend to be more generalized,
to carry less a sense of a place with cultural values.

Beginning, however, with his travels to Liberia in
1934–35 and Mexico in 1938, everything changed, and
from that point forward Greene's fictional pattern was
not to alter by much in the course of his career. Each
major novel was to follow in the steps of a journey to
some foreign place. The journey to Liberia with his
cousin Barbara culminated in the travel book *Journey
without Maps* (1936) and in a lifelong love affair with
Africa, and, later, the immensely popular novel, *The
Heart of the Matter*. His journey to Mexico resulted in *The
Lawless Roads* (1939; American title *Another Mexico*) and
shortly after that in *The Power and the Glory* (1940; first
American title, *The Labyrinthine Ways*). Greene's travel
at a climactic moment in the history of the struggle over

Indochina produced four years later *The Quiet American* (1955), a book remarkably prescient both in its view of the political situation and its analysis of American participation in the coming debacle in Vietnam. Brief trips to Cuba combined with Greene's experiences in MI6 produced the comic masterpiece on spying, *Our Man in Havana* (1958). In *A Burnt-out Case* (1961) Greene returned once again to Africa, specifically to a leper colony in the Congo, for a deeply sensitive portrayal of a man burdened by loss of faith, trying to find peace in the act of ministering to the hopeless and incurable. Greene's last three major books complete the return to foreign settings: *The Comedians* (1966), set in Haiti; *The Honorary Consul* (1973), set in Paraguay; and *The Human Factor* (1978), set in England but drawing on events that occurred at a period earlier in the novel in South Africa.

The point is not just to admire this plenitude and versatility but to understand why it is that Greene chooses to set his stories in exotic locales. Part of the reason can be seen in his debt to Conrad, for like Conrad in *Heart of Darkness,* Greene finds his most meaningful stories in the clash between the Western-English values of his protagonists as they react to cultures greatly different from their own and in exploitive political systems at odds with the cultures they rule. Uprooted by choice or chance, his protagonists confront the rootlessness of their lives. Greene is of writers often the most morally demanding, sometimes stridently so. On one level his characters are typically caught in a conflict of cultures and political values, but, deeper, they find themselves humbled by the wisdom and spirituality of the native Cubans, Haitians, Liberians, Congolese, and Vietnamese, who have an almost mystical sense of the way things really are.

Crucial to Greene's fiction too is a sense of story, of adventure. In fact, this has had as much to do with Greene's enduring popularity as has any quality in his work, and in that regard puts him somewhat at odds with the modernist tradition, where plot tends to be subordinate to character formation, where states of mind and epistemological development, or the internal drama, take precedence over the external narrative. Greene acknowledges often his indebtedness to the adventure novel, particularly to the romance tradition of Sir Walter Scott as it was inherited by Robert Louis Stevenson and H. Rider Haggard. From Greene one can always count on a compelling story. Oddly enough, it was probably his interest in the novel of intrigue––or, as he labeled it, the entertainment—that encouraged him to be a consummate storyteller.

With the dismal failure of his second and third novels, *The Name of Action* and *Rumour at Nightfall*, Greene became desperate. He was heavily in debt to his publishers and needed a quick success, and out of that need, inspired by a part-way ticket on the Orient Express and by listening to Arthur Honegger's musical suite *Pacific 231* while he composed the story, Greene was able to spin out a Balkan thriller of intrigue and deception. *Stam-*

UNDERSTANDING GRAHAM GREENE

boul Train was born. Though Greene continues to be critical of these entertainments, they are in many ways as artfully done and to be taken as seriously as his "novels."

Greene's approach to plot utilizes Dickensian as well as Haggardian elements and hinges on an Aristotelian idea of *kinesis*, or action, in which the plot begins in the middle of a problem and moves toward resolution. What distinguishes the entertainment from the novel is that in the entertainment there is solution with resolution; in the novel there is only resolution, a sense that the action is at an end, though the problem remains unsolved.

By far the most recurrent pattern in the action is that of pursuit, of someone on the run. So Pinkie and Rose do their best to escape Colleoni and his gang in *Brighton Rock*, the whisky priest tries to elude the civil authorities in *The Power and the Glory*, Charlie Fortnum hopes to escape the terrorists in *The Honorary Consul*, Maurice Castle is desperate to escape MI6 and find sanctuary in Moscow in *The Human Factor*. In the entertainment the pattern is toward success and escape (and hence a certain feeling of unreality) and in the novel toward failure and a resultant loss of freedom but a heightened sense of tragedy—though Greene's heroes inevitably fall short of tragic stature, with the exception perhaps of the whisky priest.

All-important to Greene are his characters. To better understand his approach to character development

VISTA

one needs to consider Greene's deep interest in psychoanalysis, in the unconscious, in dreams as revelations of inner lives. One cannot point to some crucial moment in Greene's development to find this strong interest in characters; it is there in the earliest work, in his first novel, *The Man Within,* in which the protagonist Andrews is torn apart by having to betray his friends. If in every Greene novel there is a macrocosmic world of the Englishman caught in native and hence alien culture, there is also a microcosmic world in which the character, usually male, is at war with himself—"There's another man within me that's angry with me," as the epigraph reads that Greene chose from Sir Thomas Browne for his first novel. All Greene's protagonists suffer from this war with self—Pinkie in *Brighton Rock,* the whisky priest in *The Power and the Glory,* Major Scobie in *The Heart of the Matter,* Querry in *A Burnt-out Case,* Castle in *The Human Factor.* There is no escape from it.

True to his early preoccupation with psychoanalysis Greene proves to be a somewhat orthodox Freudian/ Jungian. The conflicts often reveal themselves in dreams, and dreams become a key to one's understanding, though like their real-life counterparts these dreams do not always yield to interpretation easily, and they would give Freud and Jung much to ponder. Greene's narrative technique is influenced by surrealism, where the artist attempts to explore the unconscious through the evocation of dream states and dreams. Greene himself kept a dream diary for many years, then stopped, and recently has resumed it, and his early experience with psychoanalysis at the hands of Kenneth Richmond has put him among the psychological novelists.[4]

Greene would be the first to admit his debt to Henry James for providing him with models for the psychological novel; secondly, his debt is to Ford Madox Ford. He has written on James and Ford, has edited Ford, and mentions having read *The Good Soldier* several times over and learned much about narrative technique from it. The result in the novels is a sophisticated attention to point of view and a highly skilled use of it, if in fact at times an obsession with it. Within Greene's work one can find any number of variations in technique, from the rapidly shifting third-person point of view of *Brighton Rock* to the focused use of first person in *The Third Man*, where that use of point of view is transferred to the film screen as well, and then is perfected in *The End of the Affair* and *The Quiet American*.

Although Greene despairs of the label "Catholic novelist," it is not possible to disregard the iconology of Catholicism which informs his work. Not to understand the conflicts of characters as they connect to their crises of faith would be to miss the point of much of his work. As Greene himself remarks, he has always been, from the beginning of his career, a novelist who happens to be a Catholic; but it is only from *Brighton Rock* forward that understanding Catholicism and the conflicts engendered in characters who are often obsessed with matters of faith is crucial to understanding Greene. Once again, however, readers will find that, properly understood, the conflicts of faith that Pinkie, the whisky priest, Scobie, and Querry experience allow Greene to make more compelling their struggles and to make more credible their efforts to work through the problems of a dead or dying faith or to rise above a narrow Catholicism to one that is rich in its humanizing possibilities. To reject Greene as all incense and Jansenism (the seventeenth-century Catholic belief in predestination) is to miss ways in which he makes religion a crucial if not all-encompassing influence in the lives of many of his characters.

Some final remarks about Greene's style. He has admitted to being dominated in the early novels by the luxuriance of Conrad's prose, but after those excesses he soon settled into a style well honed, lapidary, almost journalistic at times, a style learned not only from great writers but also from years of copy-editing the work of others, as he did during the time he spent as subeditor on the *Times*, and from his years doing interminable reports for MI6, or writing accounts of unrest and war in faraway places like Kenya, Malaya, Indochina, and other trouble spots in the Third World. A fine introduction to the salient qualities of Greene's style is given by Samuel Hynes.[5] Hynes points specifically to Greene's precision, sense of pace, ability to heighten by understatement without losing anything to a lack of clarity. While not a minimalist, nevertheless by the height of his career Greene had developed a style that focused on the reportorial, on seeing not through the omniscient narrator but through the minds of his characters, by exploring their skill at perceiving the events they play out and their ability to apprehend and comprehend their environments, whether they be male or female, adult or child.

Some of Greene's work habits explain his crafts-manly ways. Up until recently it had been his habit to produce at least five hundred words a day, working always in the morning, in manuscript, then revising, and finally sending the copy off for typing and further revision. Lately he has reduced his output to three hundred words, still done in manuscript in an almost inde-cipherable tiny hand, then recorded on tape and sent to England for typing. An exception, but a remarkable one, was his simultaneous writing of *The Confidential Agent* and *The Power and the Glory*, the former being written in the mornings at breakneck speed in a period of about six weeks, the latter in the afternoons over several months. It was only by taking Benzedrine that Greene could keep to the pace, at great personal cost to his health and his marriage.[6]

This then is Graham Greene's craft and his fictive universe seen at a glance. It remains now to look closely at some of his best and most representative work to appreciate and understand better how the craft and con-cerns figure forth in his books.

VISTA

Notes

1. Greene states he was fifteen at the time. Norman Sherry argues for sixteen, *The Life of Graham Greene* (New York: Viking, 1989) 1: 92.

2. Material on Greene's life after 1932 is taken from *Ways of Escape* (London: Bodley Head, 1980), a loosely constructed collection of autobiographical essays, many of which have appeared as introductions to individual volumes of the Bodley Head Collected Edition of Greene's works.

3. Greene has written an essay on his early reading, "The Lost Childhood," *Collected Essays* (London: Bodley Head, 1969) 13–19.

4. Marie-Françoise Allain, *The Other Man: Conversations with Graham Greene* (New York: Simon and Schuster, 1983) 141.

5. Samuel Hynes, *Graham Greene: A Collection of Critical Essays* (Englewood Cliffs, NJ: Prentice-Hall, 1973) 5–7.

6. *Ways of Escape* 93.

CHAPTER TWO

The Early Novels

It's a Battlefield

In several ways Greene's early career serves as a model of the experiences of the beginning writer. His first two novels have never seen publication, seemingly an expense of spirit but one that over time may have proved its worth. With his third, *The Man Within*, Greene became a "new talent." Then followed a few perilous years when he saw two weak novels published and fail, and another popular book, *Stamboul Train*, only just help keep him afloat and add little to his reputation. Anguishing as this experience may have been—the two unpublishable manuscripts, the two books that were failures—they all must be counted to have figured in one way or another in Greene's first solid achievement, *It's a Battlefield*, published in 1934. Greene notes that it was the wrong book at the wrong time in his career, but in other ways it was the book that had to be written then.[1] Born of Greene's developing interest in the political novel, which he ventured into in *Stamboul Train*, and of his own growing interest in politics (he had joined the Communist Party for a brief few weeks in 1923), this novel is very much a product of the 1930s. Its reputation, however, has been unimpressive, but undeservedly so, for in many ways it is one of his strongest novels in its thematic strength, its imaginative use of form and skillfully drawn characters.

The battlefield in question is London of the 1930s, a darkling plain with ignorant armies and alarums of struggle and flight—Communist Party meetings, capitalist prison-factories, bourgeoisie fighting working class, upper class versus lower.

At a communist rally in Hyde Park a young bus driver, Jim Drover, stabbed and killed a policeman, one Arthur Coney (Greene's names often take on allegorical meaning: Drover, Conder, Coney, Surrogate, for example, in this novel), whom Drover thought was about to attack his wife, Milly. At the opening of the narrative Drover has been tried, found guilty, and sentenced to death. It only remains for the Home Secretary, in what is clearly a political and not a judicial act, to decide whether Drover's sentence should be commuted to life. The issues at the opening of the story are, Is there going to be civil unrest over the Drover affair? If so, should his sentence be reduced, most likely to eighteen years' imprisonment, to avoid trouble? The answer, coming in the course of the novel, is that there is almost no interest in Drover's plight and that it really doesn't matter much to anyone what Drover's fate will be.

UNDERSTANDING GRAHAM GREENE

The novel then develops through a series of cinematically derived shifts, using third-person point of view, from character to character (there are at least seven different points of view); two people share the largest portion of the narrative: the pursuer, Conrad Drover, brother to Jim, and the pursued, a nameless Assistant Commissioner of police, a man of fifty-six years, close to retirement after a successful career somewhere in the British Empire in the "East." The literary parent of this novel several critics have pointed out to be Joseph Conrad's *The Secret Agent.* Parallels between the two are numerous.[2]

This often confusing cinematic montage of experiences is a remarkable effort to represent the structure of the novel as a kind of "figure in the carpet," to quote Henry James's famous metaphor for describing the development of a narrative and the reader's comprehension of it. In fact, in the novel, at its very opening, the Assistant Commissioner pauses before a shop window to gaze at a carpet. He can judge its authenticity but confesses he has no understanding of its aesthetic qualities. *It's a Battlefield* suggests something of this Jamesian technique, though admittedly it is not accomplished with the same Jamesian craftsmanship. But as one walks across the carpet of the novel, the closer one gets to the end the more one is aware of a pattern and can see the whole, in this instance not just the whole carpet but the whole battlefield, where people are too indifferent or self-absorbed to care what happens to Jim Drover, except for his brother Conrad, whose motives proceed out of a need to atone for his guilt at seducing Jim's wife.

Greene's intent is to bring these two strangers, Conrad Drover and the Assistant Commissioner, from a chance encounter to a point of confrontation. At the opening of the novel Conrad Drover is the unnamed clerk who overhears the Assistant Commissioner and the Minister's secretary laughing, to him seemingly callously, over some joke about a pram being put on top of a taxi. To Conrad the experience becomes symbolic of the lack of concern of everyone, but particularly of the powers that be, about his brother's plight, and he determines to be revenged. Conrad, a hapless insurance clerk, increasingly Kafkaesque as the novel develops, sets out to make the establishment pay and to atone for his own sin. Unwittingly the Assistant Commissioner becomes one of many Greene characters who are the object of a hunt, a pursuit. This pursuit ends in Conrad Drover's failed attempt to assassinate the Assistant Commissioner and in Conrad's death. The novel closes with Jim's sentence being commuted to eighteen years, in spite of Conrad's efforts to free him, and the commutation turns out to be a fate worse than death, leaving no one satisfied.

Characteristic of the way in which Jim Drover's fate is of little consequence is the Assistant Commissioner's approach to it. He finds it a nuisance; it gets in the way of his wish to settle two other notorious cases, which he much prefers to deal with since they are puzzles to be solved and lack the moral perplexities of the Drover case. One is the Ruttledge case, so named after a suspect erroneously arrested for the brutal murder and dismemberment of an elderly lady, Mrs. Crowle, whose body is packed into a truck and left at Paddington Station. In the course of the novel this case comes to be solved, and the murderer, a religious crackpot (a Salvation Army member) is apprehended by the Assistant Commissioner. The second case is the Streatham murder, a rape-killing of one Flossie Matthews on Streatham Common. Both cases constitute intricate parts of the pattern, appearing and reappearing to capture the Assistant Commissioner's attention and provide him with welcome distractions from his assignment to advise the Minister on the Drover case. In the very last lines of the novel the Assistant Commissioner is seen, aware of the desultorily tragic end to the Drover case but suddenly exhilarated by a flash of understanding that allows him to solve the Streatham murder, a much more satisfying business to him than the muddle of the sordid, politically motivated Drover affair.

Amid this story of urban dreariness there are glimpses of a brighter world, but they are limited to a wild drive in the country through villages to the northwest of London by the two lovers, Jules Briton and Kay Rimmer, sister to Milly Drover. Even that affair ends in an abrupt and typically unsatisfying sexual encounter. Otherwise the novel offers cold comfort. In many ways it presages much of the tone of English fiction of the

THE EARLY NOVELS

1970s and 80s, particularly the novels of Margaret Drabble.

Above all, class and class matters come in for their share of satire. Queen Mary brings traffic to a halt in Regent Street when she arrives at the cinema, glimpsed by Milly and Conder as nothing but a towering head in a gray toque moving through the crowd. Home Secretary Beale is only concerned about what the populace think. Of the remaining bourgeoisie, the others are minimally admirable. The Assistant Commissioner wishes to focus only on professional competence, not on justice. In fact, he considers himself rather bad at dealing with justice. Caroline Bury, the wealthy supporter of artistic and socialist-communist causes, whom Greene modeled after Lady Ottoline Morrell, wishes to deal with problems only in an abstract manner, in an effort to satisfy her own whim, which she equates with having faith, faith being a faith in getting your own way, whatever it may be. Drover's plight is unacceptable to her as a self-evident truth, not on moral grounds but because she has decided it to be so; not because it is an offense to morality but because, in her word, it is "absurd."

Most devastating is Greene's portrayal of the smug, morally bankrupt Philip Surrogate, based loosely on John Middleton Murry, the author-critic and husband of Katherine Mansfield. Surrogate is a longtime Communist, author of numerous weighty books on socioeconomic issues, widower of Margaret, a talented artist who always saw through his pretenses. Surrogate pursues his Marxist ideals in an opulent bourgeois apartment, replete with lavish pink semicircular bed, luxurious furniture, tonily decorated rooms, served by a valet who despises him.

Much can be learned about the "battlefield" by looking at those who are the foot soldiers, the clerks or white-collars and the proles. Of the latter, the policeman-victim Arthur Coney turns out to be a hot-tempered wife abuser. His widow is a pleasant but fearful, narrow-minded, weak-willed woman. Of the servant class there is surly, disrespectful Mrs. Simpson, housekeeper to the Assistant Commissioner, and Davis, the equally iconoclastic valet to Mr. Surrogate. And of course there is Bennett, devoted but tiresome Communist Party devotee, without whom no political movement can count for much.

More deeply and sympathetically portrayed is Kay Rimmer, sister to Milly Drover, laborer in a matchbox factory. Kay is a free spirit, living for the day, not worried about narrow issues of morality, sexually promiscuous and indiscriminate. She uses Surrogate sexually, yet enjoys the freedom of her relationship with her lover Jules Briton. She feels compassion for Jim Drover's plight but knows well enough that there are limits to what one can feel. Greene, in portraying her, was looking far forward into future stories and novels. She anticipates the hedonism of Kate Farrant in *England Made Me* and Ida

THE EARLY NOVELS

Arnold in *Brighton Rock*, and shares with Kate her independence of spirit.

Of the white-collar class is Conder the newspaperman, who invents a protective domestic life of wife and six kids but lives a bachelor existence over a cafe. Conder's life is an elaborate sham. He pretends also to be a Communist but uses his contacts there to get leads for stories. He pursues the Drover case out of a sense of moral obligation but knows it isn't newsworthy and in fact is told by his editor to drop it. As a "voice" in the novel, next to those of the Assistant Commissioner and Conrad Drover, Conder's is the most intriguing because of the reportorial skills Greene has vested in him, which make him a careful observer. In his portrayal of Conder, Greene had the obvious advantage of his experiences working for the *Nottingham Journal* and the *Times*. He has Conder's measure exactly.

By far the most telling portrait is that of Conrad Drover, communist-sympathizer insurance clerk who worked his way into the official world by the possession of a gift, intelligence, of which he almost seems ashamed. For a dedicated party worker Conrad has more than his of old-fashioned bourgeois guilt, Christian-style. His love for his brother, his class hatred, his feeling of sinfulness—all combine to make him a potentially dangerous instrument; but compared to his brother, who could take up a weapon and kill cleanly, Conrad is a dismal failure. Yet to read through Conrad's passages is to begin a journey through a world of inner consciousness that Greene repeats in almost all his other protagonists, for while Drover seems ineffectual and unstable, as a psychological study he must be counted a success. Greene's art has moved beyond the repetitions in his portrayal of Andrews in *The Man Within* and the unsubtle analyses of Dr. Czinner in *Stamboul Train.* In the later pages of *It's a Battlefield* the tempo increases rapidly, as Greene takes readers deeper and deeper into Conrad's paranoia, his brilliant but increasingly unstable mind. Greene acknowledges the high quality of the final pages of the novel by characterizing them as the best he's written.[3]

In spite of weaknesses, false steps, *It's a Battlefield* continues to grow in stature. It must be counted Greene's first ambitious achievement, and points toward the themes of betrayal and atonement yet to be explored more thoroughly and expertly in novels still to be written.

England Made Me (The Shipwrecked)

Following close upon the publication of *It's a Battlefield* came *England Made Me*, Greene's next major novel, the plot of which begins in London but moves swiftly to its full setting, Stockholm. While in *It's a Battlefield* Greene explores the 1930s scene of worker unrest and

THE EARLY NOVELS

civil uprisings, in *England Made Me* he focuses on international finance and capitalism. The story is about a twin brother and sister, Anthony and Kate Farrant, and their incestuous love. One can quickly locate their literary forebears in two brother-sister pairings that reflect the two equally strong themes in their relationship. The one is that of John Ford's famous Jacobean tragedy, *'Tis Pity She's a Whore*, in which a brother and sister are obsessed with each other and bring disaster upon themselves and many others through that obsession. The other, closer to present times, is that of Charles Dickens's *Hard Times*, in which Louisa and Tom Gradgrind provide an additional pattern for Kate and Anthony. In Dickens's story Louisa is so solicitous of Tom's welfare that she willingly contrives a disastrous marriage with Josiah Bounderby, Coketown's captain of industry, so that Tom can make his way in the world as an employee at Bounderby's mill. Kate Farrant is willing to exploit her relationship with the Swedish financier—tycoon Erik Krogh, whose mistress she has become and to whom she is to be married later in the novel—so that Anthony can succeed; and she carries an overpowering love for Anthony in the same way Annabella does for her brother Giovanni in *'Tis Pity*. In addition Greene explores further the psychology of twinness—the extraordinary feelings of closeness, of like-mindedness to the point of clairvoyance, a theme he had used earlier in his short story "The End of the Party."[4] In that story Greene describes in detail the telepathic relationship a set of child twins share and the tragic outcome of that shared consciousness. The story provided a pattern for the same qualities in Kate and Anthony.

To understand what Greene was exploring in *England Made Me*, one must recognize first what is intended in this novel's original title, which was changed to an even less impressive and more confusing one—*The Shipwrecked*—in its publication in a later edition in 1953.[5] The title is an elliptical statement that might be expanded and understood in two senses, both applicable to Anthony, but also to Kate and to the other English characters in the novel: "England made me what I am" and "England made me do what I have done in my life." Anthony is at the center of the novel, a tarnished figure, anticipating many qualities to be found in later protagonists: seediness, lack of purpose, inability to settle down, an easygoing morality. Like Graham's eldest brother, Herbert, from whom much of the character of Anthony is drawn, he is a genuinely likable, warm-hearted person but also a failure. The title seems a parody of the opening lines of a famous elegy sonnet by the sixteenth-century poet Henry Howard, Earl of Surrey, on Thomas Clere, Earl of Clermont: "Norfolk sprung thee, Lambeth holds thee dead." At the close of the novel one can say about Anthony, "England made thee, Sweden holds thee dead."

In the sense that Anthony is an Englishman he is a failure, for he has been taught to worship the icons of English respectability, though they have become timeworn—the old school tie (he wears a Harrow tie, a fraudulent act, for he attended a minor public school) and a Victorian paterfamilias who beat him, expected much of him, preached to him of his duty. He seeks his fortune in places beyond the borders of England, in Shanghai, Bangkok, Aden, only to be sacked from post after post and have to depend on the kindness of his sister and her influence with Krogh. English "types" abound in the novel, typically unable to deal with the real world. They are all getting by, living shallow lives, maintaining the old forms.

Most devastating but highly entertaining is Greene's portrayal of Ferdinand Minty, a journalist who dogs Krogh's steps. Greene himself admits that Minty, once he asserted himself in the narrative, could not be controlled, much in the way Mr. Surrogate did in *It's a Battlefield*.[6] Minty's Harrovian Anglo-Catholic wealthy-mum-in-the-West-End origins contrast with his pitiful existence: the shabby clothes, cold-water walk-up, meals from tins, single teacup and spoon. Greene had already predicted Minty not only in Surrogate but also in Conder, the journalist of *It's a Battlefield*, and Minty joins Conder in the ranks of those to come in Greene's novels, those journalists pursuing their shabby profession.

The real failing in the Farrants, and in the English generally, is that they have no sense of purpose; they drift from day to day and job to job committed to a way of life that is past. They are overwhelmed by the new ways of international finance represented by Krogh, who is culturally and socially inept but a formidable power broker unfettered by any sense of the "done thing" or "fair play" or even national allegiance. The one English who is able to adapt to Krogh's ethics is Fred Hall, but he is different from the others. Hall, a Cockney, is totally a tool of Krogh's, devoted to Krogh's ends, with no sense of allegiance to anything in England's green and pleasant land.

The novelistic technique of *England Made Me* is similar to that of *It's a Battlefield*, but although Greene exhibits a surer hand in his character/observers in this novel, it lacks something of the excitement and pace of *It's a Battlefield*. Again, the reader is carried through the narrative by being attached to various characters, technically a third-person-limited point of view; the major ones are Kate and Anthony, and to a lesser extent Krogh and Minty. Within their experiences Greene also employs stream of consciousness in two memorable sections of the novel, one for Kate, one for Anthony, in which our understanding of their background is advanced considerably. The novel sets a pattern that has not altered much in the remainder of Greene's career: a story offered in larger sections (in this novel seven) divided into brief, tightly developed subsections (approximately four per section). Since, as is Greene's custom, the characters create from themselves the matter of the novel, an effective way of appreciating its artistry and thematic development is to take a close look at them.

Greene has confessed that Erik Krogh never succeeded in coming to life, and most critics agree. He is based rather closely on Ivar Kreuger, the Swedish "match king," who built an enormous financial empire which collapsed in the crash of 1929. Three years later, and three years before the publication of *England Made Me*, Kreuger committed suicide in Paris at the age of fifty-two. Krogh has risen to power in a similar way, moving from peasant origins in the rural town of Vatten, spending some years kicking about as a construction worker in Chicago, and finally finding a financial gold mine in the invention of a mechanical device referred to as the "cutter," the exact nature of which is never revealed. Krogh is intended to represent all that Anthony Farrant is not. He is a law unto himself, uncultured, introverted, amoral, willful, a true success where Anthony is a sham. Krogh's invention is a genuine success, while Anthony's silly efforts at getting rich quick are ludicrous, especially his great achievement, the handwarmer-umbrella. Krogh's possibilities for development are so apparent that one wants him to be more aggressive, more of a presence in the conflict. Greene seems to alternate between shaping a robber baron and a sentimental dotard. Yet the point is made clear through Krogh's sections that this new world of finance respects no national boundaries, involves enormous sums, places enormous faith in credit, in illusion. Behind the drama of Anthony, Kate, and Krogh there is being played out a game of risk involving the movement of huge blocks of power and money among various international corporate entities, and Krogh shows that he is a true Machi-avellian who can manipulate without concern for the little guy and keep his head through it all.

The polar opposite of Krogh, and yet one who fancies he knows what makes Krogh what he is, is Anthony Farrant. Where Krogh is a new man, bred in obscurity, rising from the proletariat, uneducated but possessed of extraordinary powers of intellect, Anthony is quite another type. He issues from late Victorian English middle-class dutifulness and complacency. In his one effort to rebel against that background he meets with his sister Kate at two o'clock in the morning in a barn not far from the down-at-heels public school he attends, and Kate convinces him not to run away but to go back and follow the respectable path. Anthony of course turns out a conventional English failure. He is one of many failed Englishmen Greene and others have portrayed. Where Anthony plays the game as a game, Krogh plays it for keeps. Anthony's sense of failure is innate and coexists with a foolish optimism, but one knows that underneath it all he understands that he has failed. His successes are puny: winning a vase and stuffed tiger at a shooting gallery in Tivoli, seducing the all-too-willing Lucia Davidge ("All Coventry was in her gesture" [153]), and most pathetic of all, winning at poker when doing so means that he certainly will have to be murdered.

It is the theme of incest, however, that tests Anthony and Kate and reveals how different they are from

THE EARLY NOVELS

each other, even though they are twins—Kate being a few minutes older than Anthony, but a few minutes that make all the difference. It is this theme that defines Kate Farrant. "[Tony's] was the weakness that should have been hers," Kate muses (166), a comment that goes to the heart of the novel. Kate's early failures first to please her father, then at nursing, her last chance at success at Hammond's secretarial school in Leather Lane, where she is discovered by Krogh—all lead to her focus on Anthony, her commitment to make him be what she wants. The situation is reminiscent in several ways of Shakespeare's *Antony and Cleopatra*, where Cleopatra is intent on creating an Antony that satisfies her needs ("I dream'd there was an Emperor Antony: / O! such another sleep, that I might see / But such another man" [V.2.76–78]). A lifetime of doing for Anthony has led Kate finally to frank admission that she is hopelessly in love with him. Anthony knows this very well but rebuffs her love out of a shallow sense of scruples, at other times from plain obtuseness. Kate is willing to defy convention and taboo, tells Anthony at one point that she is sterile, that nothing stands in their way, that she is willing for his sake to lead the double life of wife to Krogh and lover to him. In an allusion to the story of Gyges and the ring from Plato's *Republic*, Kate wishes she could twist Krogh's ring on her finger so she could change everything to suit herself. In a sense this is the course she follows, but Anthony is not up to the test, and her efforts go for nothing. She is left at the end having to pick up the pieces and move on with her life, now that Anthony is dead and the marriage to Krogh is off. She moves on, and signals that somehow the fatal bond with Anthony has been broken. She remarks that she heard nothing, felt nothing at the moment of Anthony's death, a remarkable occurrence, since prior to this event Anthony and Kate had shared a twincentered clairvoyance. She at least was always able to know or feel what he was doing or thinking. The episode signals the true death of Anthony to Kate. He failed her, could not put the conventional life behind, could not join her, even as Shakespeare's Antony could find greatness only in being lifted up in the act of dying to Cleopatra's level, on her monument.

In spite of some clear flaws *England Made Me* is a remarkable book, for its frank treatment of incest, for its extraordinary story, and for its inventiveness and unusual handling of the theme of betrayal. Anthony does not betray Kate in the way Conrad Drover betrayed his brother Jim, but his failure, when so much is demanded of him, is a betrayal nonetheless, and Greene shows the weaknesses inherent in Anthony as representative of an England that is out of date, far gone, in a modern world.

THE EARLY NOVELS

Brighton Rock

Of all Greene's novels *England Made Me* strikes many readers as his most secular, most devoid of religious issues and the iconology of faith. With the exception of Ferdinand Minty's rarified Anglo-Catholicism, religion does not figure at all in the novel. *Brighton Rock,* however, was to change all that for good. To understand fully this brilliant and aggressively moral tale from Greene's early career, one needs to recognize that it participates heavily in allegory. In that sense Greene is working within a literary tradition as old as literature itself and a tradition of interpretation that sees meaning on at least two and often several levels. In allegory a narrative means both what it says in a literal sense and "something else" in a spiritual or symbolic sense. The word *allegory* derives from the Greek *allegoria*, deriving in turn from two Greek roots, *allos* ("other") and *agoria* ("speaking").[7] So to "speak other" means to give rise to deeper and fuller meanings out of the "facts" of the narrative. The problem for the reader is to take "the fruit and lat the chaf be stille"—take the fruit and leave the chaff alone, as Geoffrey Chaucer's Nun's Priest tells the pilgrims at the close of his sermon. When one understands that *Brighton Rock* is an allegory—or, to use a medieval term, a modern *psychomachia*, a struggle of the soul for salvation—and that Brighton, the tawdry but alluring seaside resort, is the world, and that the characters in it are participating in a powerful modern morality play, with salvation hovering at its center, just as it does in a morality play like *Everyman*, then one can appreciate all the more the artistry of this novel.[8]

Two aspects of what allegory is not need to be stressed. Allegory is not a mathematical working out of signifier-signified in a codelike translation of literal meaning to allegorical or spiritual meaning. Allegory consists of a loose, open-ended relationship between literal and spiritual, just as it is to a greater or lesser extent in the works of the master poets of allegory, Dante and Edmund Spenser, in the *Divine Comedy* and *The Faerie Queene*, and in more recent writers like Franz Kafka and Flannery O'Connor, where allegory is integral to their narratives. One needs to be warned away from allegorical labels for Pinkie and Rose and Ida; they are not simply Damnation, Salvation, and the Worldly, although they partake of these qualities. Likewise, one needs to remember that in all narratives of a figural kind (and some critics would argue that all narratives are to a greater or lesser extent figural) the figural cannot exist without the truth of the literal, that one cannot exploit Pinkie or Rose or Ida, for example, for their allegorical significations and abandon them as people. They are persons and significations at one and the same time, just as Brighton is Brighton, a geographical and temporal entity, and a symbolic entity at one and the same time. Once properly understood, a sense of the allegorical significance in *Brighton Rock* can lead to a deeper understanding of its import.

THE EARLY NOVELS

As with the two earlier novels a key to understanding this novel is first to understand its title. *Brighton Rock* of course refers first of all to the resort town on the south coast of England, about fifty miles south of London. Brighton rock is a kind of hard candy sold throughout Brighton; it is cylindrical in form, about eight inches in length, and varies in diameter. It is white in color, with a pink "rind," and in pink the word *BRIGHTON* appears on the ends of the cylinder and through it, no matter where it is cut or broken. As candy it is the instrument of Hale's death at the beginning of the novel, as he is killed when Pinkie and his thugs shove a stick of rock down his throat, which brings on the heart attack that kills him.[9] The candy also functions as a form of the phallus and as a metaphor for human nature. It is also the first wedding gift from Pinkie to Rose, when he buys two sticks of rock after the civil ceremony, and they stand sucking them before they go back to Frank's and to their marriage bed. The sticks are probably ones left from a box from which the rock used to kill Hale was taken. Brighton rock is a symbol of human nature, for as Ida says break it anywhere and it's always the same—but perhaps with a difference, since it is the colors of purity and hope and possibly of salvation, of the names of Greene's two wisely innocent ones, Pinkie and Rose.

More symbolic of the world at large is the resort city in which Greene sets his story—Brighton. While in the earlier two novels Greene had used settings to effect—

UNDERSTANDING GRAHAM GREENE

London in *It's a Battlefield* and Stockholm in *England Made Me*—they do not compare to what Greene achieves with Brighton. It is Brighton on Whit Monday, the day after Pentecost, on Bank Foliday, a festive Monday. Brighton is an amalgam of the whole world as it appears at its gaudiest. Critics characterize Greene's Brighton as dark and demonic, but in truth it can be the opposite; it is threateningly gaudy, at turns bizarre and mournful, at turns dangerous. It, in the words of Walt Whitman, is large, contains multitudes, and certainly contradictions. Greene himself says that he thought his treatment of Brighton in the novel was a labor of love, not hate.[10] Brighton holds pathetic old people like Rose's mean parents, and also the hag who sits in an alley saying the rosary. It holds common hoods like Dallow and Cubitt, criminal tycoons like Colleoni, upper-class snobs like the girls playing games on the public school fields or the two patrician sparks who come into the hotel and ogle Rose. It holds the lush Cosmopolitan hotel, Frank's seedy house, and the fussy restaurant, Snow's, from which Rose is dismissed. It contains also desolate Nelson Place, the ghetto from which Rose comes, and Pinkie's destroyed home, Paradise Piece. Whatever it may or may not be, it is the world represented on holiday, attracting to it the great mass of humanity, all of life teeming and, like Ida, always hoping for a bit of fun.

Somewhere deep within Brighton can be found Pinkie and Rose, who are "real Brighton" and who would feel out of place anywhere else, while Ida is an

THE EARLY NOVELS

interloper, a Londoner down from her digs behind Russell Square. Pinkie and Rose move to the ubiquitous mournful music of Brighton—the lone violin always playing above the sound of the sea, Ida Arnold's snatches of ballads and bawdy songs, the bands playing, gramophones playing—suggestive of the ever-present music on Shakespeare's uninhabited island in *The Tempest*. Pinkie, restless in the presence of the music of Brighton, is the Caliban whom Miranda embraces rather than spurns. Beyond Brighton, as also in *It's a Battlefield* and *England Made Me*, there is rural but equally sordid solitude. Here it is the suburb of Peacehaven, where Pinkie and Rose venture on occasions; but Peacehaven is also the place of the possible loss of Pinkie's virginity, with Spicer's girl Sylvie, and the scene of Pinkie's death. Brighton is where things are meant to happen, for as in the earlier two novels where one can always drive to the country, the country cannot heal urban wounds. Pinkie himself says you can't do anything with it. Brighton is as much the world here as Jerusalem is in the New Testament or Rome in *The City of God*; it is at once splendid, gaudy, seedy, and dangerous, but at all times fascinating, riveting.

In *Brighton Rock* one is confronted with the clash between the worldly and the spiritual, and the world nurtures those who do not, those who yearn to escape it. Such are Pinkie and Rose; Brighton-ness deserves fuller treatment once one grasps the full import of what the world signifies.

UNDERSTANDING GRAHAM GREENE

First, it signifies social difference. Greene, in a published interview, pointedly comments that he views *It's a Battlefield*, *Brighton Rock*, and *The Honorary Consul* as being tied closely together in their critique of social conditions, and that the impact of poverty on Pinkie and Rose because of their origins in the slum of Nelson Place causes *Brighton Rock* to be as much a novel of social protest as it is a religious novel.[11] Two scenes particularly focus attention on the gulf that separates upper-class life from that of most of Greene's Brighton residents. At the opening of Part Four, Greene describes the carnival atmosphere of Brighton and contrasts it with that of the girl hockey players on the public school grounds, padded like armadillos, trooping out "solemnly" to their game, watching the commoners gaily make their way to the festivities. Later, toward the end of the novel, Greene presents a devastating brief cameo of two young travelers who stop for a drink at the hotel where Pinkie and Rose have stopped. They come stomping in out of the rain in their expensive camel-hair coats, taking care to request that their lager be served in tankards. Pinkie "watched their gambits with hatred from the stairs" (297). They eye the unattractive Rose with an arrogance and sense of ownership, of *droit de seigneur*, assuming that by virtue of their rank they have a claim to her. Pinkie is so enraged he has a sudden impulse to give it all up and let Rose live, "less a motion of pity than of weariness" (298), a weariness akin to *accidia*, to being tired of the world.

THE EARLY NOVELS

Beyond these two vignettes is the prenovel existence of Pinkie, Rose, Dallow, Spicer, Cubitt, and the others. Their Brighton is the Brighton of Nelson Place, not of the resort city. Pinkie recalls the devastating childhood he spent in his home, ironically named Paradise Piece, with parents, now dead, whose affection found regular weekly expression in Saturday-night sex in a dismal flat with no privacy. More significantly, he recalls being a wandering teen orphan on the Brighton waterfront when he was adopted by Kite, possibly the only person to show any real affection toward him before he met Rose. This fact helps to explain his killing of Hale, which he saw as an act of revenge for the death of someone he obviously revered. One gets an even closer look at Rose's family when Pinkie and Rose go to Nelson Place to get her parents' permission to marry. Both father and mother prove to be sour, uncommunicative, having "got a mood." Finally they open up enough to haggle away Rose's future, a parody of the traditional dowry of the propertied class, as Pinkie is manipulated into paying them fifteen guineas for Rose's hand in marriage. Later, when Rose is dismissed from her waitressing job at Snow's, she tells Pinkie that her parents are upset with her, since she'll no longer be able to send them money. It is an old story: two young people desperate for change, thrown together, in this case at least one of them finding what she thinks is a paradise in a new life in marriage.

UNDERSTANDING GRAHAM GREENE

Except for Pinkie and Rose, and the few figures like the old lady praying the rosary and the father confessor at the close of the novel, the great mass of characters in *Brighton Rock* come to terms with Brighton, sometimes willingly, sometimes wearily. Hale's plight is fascinatingly typological to the novel, since his pursuit by the forces of death in the form of Pinkie and his gang anticipates the pursuit of Pinkie and Rose by Ida Arnold. Hale searches desperately for something in the world to save him, like the character Everyman from the medieval morality play, first with the London teen-agers on holiday, Molly Pink and Delia, finally with Ida Arnold, who in her temporary abandonment of him gives him over to death. Symptomatic of the sterility of secular life is Hale's funeral back in London. It is presided over by a preacher who drones passionlessly about Hale's being reabsorbed into the "universal spirit," as if Hale, who held on to life desperately, had any interest in an afterlife. Hale's corpse is shunted through the New Art doors of the nondenominational chapel into the fires of the crematory, and poor Ida manages to blink out "with difficulty a last tear" (40).

Others find the world decent, if not a comfort at least manageable, once one learns to get along in it. Ted Dallow, for example, seems relatively at ease in his affair with Frank's wife, Judy, in his loosely arranged and pursued life of crime. The lawyer Prewitt is less comfortable but coping in a dead marriage (his wife looks out from below ground like some character in a Beatrix

THE EARLY NOVELS

Potter story) and a tawdry legal career. He puts up a humanistic-secular barrier against the sordid world, drawing tag ends from his public school and university education, and tries pitifully to spin out a philosophy of life from misremembered quotes taken from Shakespeare, Matthew Arnold, and Robert Browning. He reminds one of Anthony Farrant of *England Made Me* as he might appear in late middle age, waiting as Anthony waits, with his idol Mr. Micawber, for something to "turn up." What turns up is Pinkie Brown. By contrast, the underworld leader Colleoni exudes comfort, ease; he has found his place and has indeed made the world his oyster. He is bound to win, Pinkie to lose. Colleoni and the ambience of the Cosmopolitan, the poshest hotel in Brighton, reflect a luxuriant sense of the world; Colleoni, like Ida Arnold, is very much in control of things.

The true *spiritus mundi*, the spirit of the world, is Ida Arnold, far more powerful and far more dangerous in her own way than Colleoni. She remains one of Greene's most memorable characters. It has been suggested that Greene's portrayal of Ida owes something to Mae West as he describes her in a review of one of her movies.[12] As was Mae West, Ida is totally at home in the world. She is in every way a creature of the world, earthbound, lifebound, smelling of Californian Poppy, a cheap perfume. She keeps a store of second-rate novelists' works on the shelves of her flat (J. B. Priestley, Edgar Wallace, Warwick Deeping; anyone can know Greene's opinion of a writer by noticing which characters read his or her books). She is physically attractive, buxom, holding on to her forty years well but not hiding them. Ida moves through the streets of London like a force; buses, cabs, pedestrians defer to her. She has no religious beliefs, holds instead with ghosts, in the spiritualism of the tabloids that shriek out their headlines about dead husbands who return to their homes to get their widows to twiddle the radio dial and tune in warning weather reports. In times of true crisis Ida turns not to religion but to the Ouija board. Being a Londoner, she brings to Brighton the matter-of-factness of London, hearty but all business, bullying poor Phil Corkery into sexual performances he is bound to fail at. Ida's ethic is one not of salvation and judgment but of duty, obligation, right and wrong, of social and moral habit. She is maternal protectiveness at its worst. She is childless, divorced from her husband yet menacingly thinking of going back to him. She seems to have no visible source of income. Her screen model is Mae West, her literary ancestor Molly Bloom of James Joyce's *Ulysses*, with whom she shares a frank and earthy sexuality, to which she adds a meddlesome morality.

Greene remarked, and critics have often felt likewise, that the first part of *Brighton Rock* ought to have been dropped, and Hale's episode worked into the remainder of the novel. However, to make such a change would be to ignore the typological relationship Hale's death has to Pinkie's, and Ida's role in it. Initially Hale and Ida are thrown together, Hale desperate for someone to protect him. Judgment—in the form of Pinkie, Cubitt, Dallow, Spicer, those four horsemen of the Apocalypse, in the form of revenge for Kite's murder—pursues Hale, and Hale fights for his life. Ida turns out to be no Rose to this Pinkie; she goes off for a wash, momentarily abandoning Hale, and Hale meets his dreadful end. When Ida gets the news of Hale's death back in London on the following Wednesday, she feels remorse and guilt. Typically egocentric, she sees Hale as abandoning *her*, can't understand why he walked off instead of waiting. But, she thinks, he did his job, such as it was, and she determines, after suitably being convinced both by her intuition and the turn at the Ouija board, to do right by him. Her actions are partly to soothe her conscience, since later she opines that if she hadn't been tipsy, Fred would never have died; but to a great extent they are prompted by pride, a love of the chase, a desire to control events, to get her way. By Part Five, Ida has trouble recalling Fred, gets his attire confused with that of Charlie Moyne. In Part Seven, the last section of the novel, Phil tells her bluntly that she's only seeking her revenge for Fred's death for the fun, that she really didn't care all that much about Fred, and she says she can't deny what he says: "What's the harm in that? I like doing what's right, that's all" (278). But Phil can see the effects of her obsession, causing further tragedy, while she sees it as one more good deed done in her life to add to her others: saving a man from drowning, giving money to a blind beggar, offering a word of comfort to a despondent young girl in the Strand. She lies, deceives people, and finally wins. The world is perhaps a securer place for Ida's having prevailed, but in a broader context her victory is hollow, unsatisfying, as unsatisfying as sex with Phil Corkery, and she knows it.

The potent waif-wife to Pinkie, Rose Wilson, could not be cast more in opposition to Ida than she is and functions in the narrative as Ida's literal and spiritual-symbolic opposite. Ida is blond; Rose mouse brown. Ida is healthy, bosomy, fortyish; Rose is anorexic, wan, a bare sixteen. Ida drinks; Rose is an abstainer. Ida is a Londoner, from Holborn; Rose native Brighton, from Nelson Place. Ida is sexually experienced; Rose a virgin. Ida appears superficially to be fertile, but is in fact infertile. Rose, however, is fertile, knows immediately after the wedding night that she is pregnant with Pinkie's child. Ida's secular-superstitious religious impulses contrast with Rose's combative, strongly held Catholic faith, which translates into her faith in and commitment to Pinkie, to which Ida's commitment to the memory of Fred Hale is a pale rival. Both struggle for Pinkie's destiny, and in a strange way both get what they want: Ida her secular justice, Rose her promise for the future, in the hope of Pinkie's salvation and in the child she carries.

The appearance of this emaciated woman-child at a little after two o'clock on a Whit Monday afternoon changes everything forever. Rose shows up shortly after Hale's murder. She holds, through her shrewd surmises, the key to Hale's death, which threatens Pinkie and forces him to consider what he can do to stifle her. The obvious solution is to kill her, but, oddly, Pinkie settles on a more bizarre plot: to marry her and then finally to trick her into a double suicide, which he plans to pull out of after she dies.

It is almost impossible to talk of Rose without talking of Pinkie. Both are teens, he seventeen, she sixteen, from the same impoverished area of Brighton. Both are "Roman," and both show the overpowering effects of the faith into which they were born. Pinkie at one time had planned to be a priest. Rose's commitment to Pinkie is a conscious act, while Pinkie's to Rose is one he struggles against constantly but finally gives in to. He marries her, consummates the marriage, impregnates her.

What Greene has done with Rose's devotion is to take the emotions of an overpowering teen-age infatuation and deepen them into a love of startling intensity and selflessness. Wandering, emotionally unmoored, Rose and Pinkie find each other in the midst of Brighton, where love seems to have died. Rose offers her third-person perspective in only two sections, while Pinkie figures in at least eighteen; but his obsession with her causes her always to be present (she appears in fourteen of them) even when she is not, and technically of course what the reader knows of Rose is heavily dependent on how Pinkie sees her. He gets her "like you get God in the Eucharist"; she is something that completes him (221). Rose's devotion to him frustrates him, but it is so overpowering he cannot break it. The more he fights it, the more he is drawn to it.

For Rose paradise in an earthly sense is marriage to Pinkie. In Part Seven, Section 1, she voices the poetry of her feelings in an aubade, or dawn song, on Sunday morning, the day after the wedding. Knowing or believing she is now in the country of mortal sin, she is amazed that she can be so incredibly happy. Yet Rose, like anyone who has partaken of a mystery (in the religious sense), cannot convey to her girlfriend Maisie at Snow's what it feels like to be married to Pinkie. " 'Oh, Rose, what's it like?' " " 'Lovely' " (242). She thinks to herself, "What have I done to deserve to be so happy?" (243). Back at Frank's, when Ida appears, the struggle between Ida and Rose over Pinkie ensues. Ida's arguments are hard to combat; people don't change; they're like the sticks of Brighton rock; it's not confession, repentance, it's "the world we got to deal with," she says (247). But in the end Rose is unmoved. Her devotion to Pinkie remains firm as ever, even firmer. Ida has lost; she has nothing. Rose has the child.

It is not Rose or Ida, however, who is the focus of *Brighton Rock*. It is the teen-age murderer Pinkie Brown. Pursued by both Ida and Rose in their own needful ways Pinkie is the object of pursuit, though he also is a pursuer. Over three-fourths of the sections of the novel are given over to his perspective. He is an orphan, taken off a Brighton pier by the gang leader Kite, whose murder at the hands of Colleoni's thugs after having been fingered by Hale precipitates the action of this novel. Pinkie has tried to fill Kite's shoes and is having difficulty proving himself. He seeks power yet is powerless. No one pays him any heed, not Colleoni, not the bookie Brewer, not the waitresses at Snow's, not the photographer who refuses to sell him Spicer's picture. His Catholicism is clearly heretical, Jansenist, Augustinian, full of damnation, where Rose's begins as one of hope. Hell lay about him in his infancy, Greene says, in mockery of Wordsworth's famous line. "'Of course there's Hell. Flames and damnation, . . . torments,'" Pinkie says. "'And Heaven too,'" Rose replies. Pinkie: "'Oh, maybe . . . maybe'" (62).

In spite of his resistance to Rose, Pinkie sees that they are two halves of one whole, like Donne's lovers in "The Sunne Rising" or "The Exstasie," whom Greene mimes in the scene in Peacehaven when Pinkie and Rose recline on the grass. They "suit each other down to the ground," Pinkie reasons, an echo of the "stirrup / ground" line from Camden's *Remains* that Pinkie and Rose mention several times. Rose "was good, he'd discovered that, and he was damned: they were made for each other" (155). Like the adolescent, innocent, virginal lovers they are, they grow together physically, sexually. Pinkie is Rose's first boy; she's the first girl he's kissed, a remarkable fact for a kid from Paradise Piece. It is apparent that they have been saved for each other. When Pinkie fully appreciates Rose's exceptional intelligence, after she admits she's figured out the mys-

UNDERSTANDING GRAHAM GREENE

tery of Kolley Kibber, he says, "You're as bad as me. There's not a pin to choose between us" (231).

Between the *spiritus mundi* (Ida) and the Paraclete, the traditional comforter (Rose) is the sinner in danger of losing his eternal soul. One cannot conceive of Pinkie Brown as anything but a religious figure from the moment he enters the story, his slim body draped ineptly in a too-large ready-made suit, his aged look, "the slatey eyes ... touched with the annihilating eternity from which he had come and to which he went" (22). He moves through Brighton with a disdain for it that is akin to *contemptus mundi*, the attitude of the desert fathers of the Early Church for the world. Nor does he have any use for the country outside it; as he comments on his and Rose's earlier visit to Peacehaven, you can't do anything with the country. There is little that separates Pinkie's virginality and asceticism from that of the religious fanatic. He has almost no interest in things; clothes hang on him; money is kept lying about in soap dishes; and he harbors a fear and loathing of sex. He had a desire at one time to be a priest. He is a firm believer. He prays in times of crisis. When presented with a *modus* for salvation he is torn between destroying it (her) and clinging to it, as he is drawn back to Rose again and again throughout the story. There is clearly more to his dependence on her than his wish to keep her mouth shut about Hale's murder.

He believes himself to be damned. Like Dr. Faustus of Christopher Marlowe's play, he cannot seem to accept the fact that God would even think of saving him. One recalls Faustus's line, "The serpent that tempted Eve may be saved, but not Faustus" (V.2.41–42). Maybe there is a heaven. Maybe "between the stirrup and the ground" a sinner can reach out to God. As Pinkie drives through Rottingdean toward Peacehaven, he mulls over the possibility: "Heaven was a word: hell was something he could trust" (284). And yet, he thinks, why should he be denied a vision of heaven, even "if it was only a crack between the Brighton walls," and looks at Rose as if she might be that vision, but it's too difficult for him to see her in that way. The inevitability of despair coexists in his mind with a sense of hope.

In the ending to this novel Greene has not disappointed readers who expect from him a cruel and breathtaking twist in the outcome. It has been described as one of the most disagreeable in modern fiction. Yet properly viewed it makes perfect sense, both the cruelty of the Orphic voice of the record Pinkie cuts for Rose and the ambiguity of Pinkie's death. Prophetically, midway in the novel, Pinkie tells Rose to "go back where you came from," a message put even more harshly on the record: "God damn you, you little bitch, why can't you go back home forever and let me be" (171, 218). The message is undeniably cruel, but it is also an anguished cry for release from pursuit by a sinner who says on the next page he'd "got [Rose] like you got God in the Eucharist—in the guts" (221). What Rose will make of this "worst horror of all" when she plays the message after

UNDERSTANDING GRAHAM GREENE

Pinkie's death is anyone's guess, though it would be difficult to see her, determined and willful as she is, take it as a rejection. Pinkie's death, the fall from the cliff after his accidental blinding, occurs in Peacehaven, at the end of a road that leads off a cliff. In Pinkie's paradigmatically tragic ending, which R. W. B. Lewis sees as parallel to that of Oedipus (though more so of Gloucester in *King Lear*, even though his fall is not fatal and is a sham), whether or not he is saved must be an open question always. One may hope that his name and Rose's signify something; one may wish that the pinkness and whiteness of Brighton rock do also. One may hope that between the edge of the cliff and the depths below he sought mercy and found it. In the final section the father confessor points clearly to a truth embraced throughout *Brighton Rock:* that no one can possibly conceive of "the . . . appalling . . . strangeness of the mercy of God" (308). The ellipses here are crucial, for even the priest has difficulty choosing the words to describe what he believes. And he also shows that in the world sinners may be clearly identified and labeled, but in the larger context of eternity, as in the example the priest uses of the French religious thinker Charles Péguy, our saints may be sinners and our sinners saints, so bound up with each other and so mysterious are the concepts of good and evil.

Brighton Rock marks a definite advance in Greene's fiction; some go so far as to say it is his best work, "a sad thought after more than thirty years," Greene com-

ments (xiii). It is particularly remarkable in its blending
of action and theme, in, to use Greene's taxonomy, a
fusion of entertainment and novel. While in some ways
the technical handling of point of view in *Brighton Rock*
shows no significant advance over that of *It's a Battlefield*
and *England Made Me*, in its pace, its use of dramatic and
real time, exploitation of the pursuit motif in several
variations, and its exceptional use of place, Greene has
created a brilliant work, perhaps his best. In its sympathy toward the characters of Pinkie and Rose and the
force of its portrayal of their squalid but highly moving
lives, Greene's handling is unrivaled. Critics and readers often bridle at the persistence of the religious allegory in the narrative, its insistence on being recognized
and given attention; but, as noted earlier, *Brighton Rock*
fuses narrative and allegory in the best way, so that they
are so firmly bound up in one another that they cannot
possibly be pried apart. True, an appreciation of the
Western allegorical tradition can enrich one's reading
of *Brighton Rock*, but even without it the novel is compelling enough to allow the story to carry its message with
relative ease. Further, in its turning to the iconology of
Catholicism and its involvement in the religious quest,
Brighton Rock predicted the future direction of Greene's
career, toward *The Power and the Glory*, *The Heart of the
Matter*, and *The End of the Affair*, all novels with strong
religious concerns, haunted by protagonists who share
much with Pinkie Brown, who almost might be thought
of as the progeny of Pinkie and Rose.

Notes

1. Introduction to *It's a Battlefield* (London: Heinemann and Bodley Head, 1970) viii.

2. See esp. Kenneth Allott and Miriam Farris, *The Art of Graham Greene* (New York: Russell and Russell, 1963) 85–100; and Lynne Cheney, "Joseph Conrad's *The Secret Agent* and Graham Greene's *It's a Battlefield*: A Study in Structural Meanings," *Modern Fiction Studies* 16 (Spring 1970): 117–31.

3. Introduction x.

4. This story appeared in the *London Mercury* 25 (Jan. 1932): 238–44, and was published in the same year as *England Made Me* in Greene's first short story collection, *The Basement Room and Other Stories* (London: Cresset, 1935) 55–72.

5. *The Shipwrecked* (New York: Viking, 1953). The title was an alternate to *England Made Me* and appears on Greene's original manuscript, dated 16 Nov. 1933, which is in the Humanities Research Center, University of Texas, Austin.

6. *England Made Me* (London: Heinemann and Bodley Head, 1970) x; further references are to this edition and are noted parenthetically.

7. For a helpful introduction to allegory see Edwin Honig, *Dark Conceit: The Making of Allegory* (New York: Oxford University Press, 1959).

8. See Robert O. Evans, "The Satanist Fallacy of *Brighton Rock*," *Graham Greene: Some Critical Considerations*, ed. Evans (Lexington: University of Kentucky Press, 1967) 164–65, and R. W. B. Lewis, "The 'Trilogy,'" *Graham Greene: A Collection of Critical Essays*, ed. Samuel Hynes (Englewood Cliffs, NJ: Prentice-Hall, 1973) 49–59. Evans has a disturbing habit of looking almost everywhere in Western literature but *Brighton Rock* itself to argue that Pinkie, like Satan, is a figure of condemnation.

9. David G. Wright, "Greene's *Brighton Rock*," *Explicator* 41 (Summer 1983): 52–53.

THE EARLY NOVELS

10. *Brighton Rock* (London: Heinemann and Bodley Head, 1970) xii; further references are to this edition and will be noted parenthetically.

11. Marie-Françoise Allain, *The Other Man: Conversations with Graham Greene* (New York: Simon and Schuster, 1983) 85.

12. Allott and Farris 150.

CHAPTER THREE

Religion and the Novel

The Power and the Glory

Brighton Rock marks a definite turn in the direction of Greene's writing. More and more he chose to view his "novels," his serious efforts, as dramas on powerful themes of faith and the world as they affect one central character and to reserve for his "entertainments" a lighter, melodramatic, action-directed kind of fiction. More importantly, he chose to write both entertainment and novel simultaneously. Illustrative of this strategy is the fact that he wrote *The Confidential Agent* (1939), one of his best-known entertainments, simultaneously with *The Power and the Glory* (1940), his most profoundly religious novel, and that from 1943 through 1961 other entertainments alternated with novels.

Greene's next major novel after *Brighton Rock* is *The Power and the Glory*, a story set in Mexico in the 1930s, about a Catholic priest seeking to escape the Red Shirts, the civil militia of the state of Tabasco. *The Power and the Glory* formed a pattern in Greene's writing career that

RELIGION AND THE NOVEL

was to recur often in future years, in which a journey to a foreign country would inspire the creation of a novel set in that land. Greene had negotiated with the publishers Longmans, Green to sponsor his journey to Mexico to report on the suppression of the Catholic Church there under the political regime of former President Plutarco Calles, particularly its aggressive implementation in Tabasco under its governor, Garrido Canabal.[1] The journey to Mexico produced Greene's second travel book, *The Lawless Roads* (American title *Another Mexico*, both published in 1939), a fascinating and painful narrative. The complementarity of *The Lawless Roads* and its fictional child *The Power and the Glory* is stronger than that of any other two of Greene's works. Scenes, events, and characters are lifted out of *The Lawless Roads* and dropped into *The Power and the Glory*, frequently with little change. The most important borrowing from *The Lawless Roads* is that of Greene's central character, the whisky priest, whom Greene caught in his mind from a casual conversation in Tabasco, where an alcoholic fugitive priest was described to him. The priest had an illegitimate daughter and was reputed to have been so drunk at a baptism that he christened a boy child Brigitta, the name of the whisky priest's daughter in the novel.[2] Greene was told that the priest had apparently disappeared into the forests of Tabasco and had never been heard of again.[3] The whisky priest's martyrdom and certain facts about his life are also drawn from the life and martyrdom of Father Miguel Pro Juárez, S.J., who was executed for treason in 1927 and whose life was well known to Greene and discussed at some length in *The Lawless Roads*. Pro was a native of Mexico but educated in the United States and Belgium. Photographs of Pro's execution were circulated widely by President Calles.[4]

Secondary to the influence of Greene's travels one can detect the deeper influence of his broad reading in religion and literature, particularly Dostoevski's *The Brothers Karamazov* and Hawthorne's *The Scarlet Letter*. Greene's scenes between the lieutenant and the whisky priest remind one of those between the prisoner and the Grand Inquisitor in *The Brothers Karamazov*, and the parallels between Arthur Dimmesdale's feelings for his illegitimate daughter Pearl and the priest's for Brigitta are readily apparent. Too, Greene was well aware of the parallels to be found between the religious persecution in Tabasco and that of Catholics in England under Queen Elizabeth I—of Edmund Campion and Robert Southwell, and the experiences of John Gerard, who managed to outlast his persecutors.[5]

In his important interview with Marie-Françoise Allain, Greene mentioned that his first act in beginning a novel is to choose a title and that the title is crucial to understanding the novel. This has already been noted in *It's a Battlefield, England Made Me,* and *Brighton Rock. The Power and the Glory* is no exception. The title is taken of course from the close of the Lord's Prayer; today the phrase is still not included in the Catholic version of the

RELIGION AND THE NOVEL

prayer but now is a part of the mass.[6] In the novel the title is both literal and ironic. Literally the *power* stands for the lieutenant, the holder of civil power, and the *glory* stands for the whisky priest, moving toward some unwanted but inevitable martyrdom. On the other hand, in an ironic sense both terms can be seen to represent the whisky priest because he represents the power of faith and the ineluctable force of God in the world, against which the temporal power of the lieutenant must fail. The structure of the novel is built around the pursuit of the priest by the lieutenant, but the outcome is ambiguous. The whisky priest is caught and executed, but at the very close of the book his place is taken by another priest. The lieutenant, on the other hand, shows definite signs of the effects of grace, and may be the Christian *malgré lui*, in spite of himself. Hence the irony: Whose is the power, whose the glory?

To understand the interplay of this power and glory one needs to envision the novel as an allegory, as with *Brighton Rock*, in which the literal experience consists of the playing out of the traditional Greene motif of pursuit; here the Tabascan state, in the persons of the lieutenant and his Red Shirts, tries to capture and kill the fugitive priest. The priest is desperately trying to do what is right, both to meet his priestly obligations and to preserve his life. In the best tradition of allegory, on the literal level Greene is always at pains to develop a strong narrative pace. On the spiritual level he deals with the profundity of "last things," of eschatology:

UNDERSTANDING GRAHAM GREENE

death, judgment, heaven, and hell, of what lies beyond the temporal and spatial boundaries of this world. Although some commentors, including George Orwell and Sean O'Faolain, are put off by the eschatological element, it is a profound concern of Greene's. Likewise, the element of the hagiological, of the tradition of the saint's life, cannot be ignored, though Greene's saint's life here operates against the grain of the hagiological tradition.[7] Hence the contrast between the saccharine tale of the young martyr Juán, whose story is read by the mother to the boy Luis and his siblings, and the revulsion Luis feels toward it. Hence too the contrast between the whisky priest, so called because of his alcoholism, and the traditional image of the ideal priest. The priest's journey is a spiritual one in the sense that he does not change fundamentally but that his true goodness comes as a gradual revelation to him and to readers through his conduct, and that at the close of this allegory the reader is wrapped in a mystery and properly in awe of the holiness of this man, a holiness that he does not choose to display but one that is innate and ineluctable.

Greene's fundamentally ascetic impulse can disturb contemporary readers who expect narratives that embrace the world more fully. *Brighton Rock*'s quarrel with the world must necessarily continue in *The Power and the Glory* and on through Greene's writings. In *The Lawless Roads* Greene communicates an undisguised hatred of Mexico—of the climate, the politics, but especially of the

RELIGION AND THE NOVEL

people: their seeming insensitivity to evil, their lack of concern over injustice, and their habit of mingling acts of simple affection and with those of unspeakable violence. Yet in *The Power and the Glory* it is the Mexican peasants who reflect the true spirit of community, while the gringos and politicos and pistoleros represent the restless world—Tench, the dentist trying to get a grip on life; the Fellowses, immature, frivolous, unable to cope; the Lehrs, the pious Lutheran brother and sister with all the answers, bullying everyone by, as their German name denotes (Lehr, from *lehren*, to teach) a teachy and meddlesome puritanism; on the Mexican side the callous Red Shirts, the self-obsessed and politic chief of police, and the mercenary mestizo.

On the other hand the children in the novel exhibit an openness and canniness unique to them, not shared by adults. The whisky priest's illegitimate daughter, Brigitta, is a sign to him of his constant failing; she lives to mock him. At the same time in Brigitta there are glimmerings of grace; she does not betray her father, as other children in Greene's stories do. He, in turn, recognizes her capacity for good and would give up his own soul to save her, a sinful act but one shared by other of Greene's characters, as we saw in Rose's love for Pinkie in *Brighton Rock*, and shall see in Scobie's actions in *The Heart of the Matter*.

Of the little Indian boy who is heartlessly killed by the Red Shirts in their attempt to capture the fugitive murderer Calver little can be said except to note the obvious way in which he is sacrificed to the world of adult justice, cruelty, and revenge. More interesting, however, is the country child Luis, whose mother reads to him and her family the life of brave young Juán. To Luis, Juán appears incredible, unreal, except for the realism of his execution. More real to him are the accouterments of power vested in the lieutenant, specifically in his gun, which early in the novel Luis is allowed to examine. At the end of the novel, however, Luis is able to recognize an authentic martyr in the whisky priest, and in spitting on the lieutenant's gun he marks his rejection of all that the lieutenant represents.

The most significant child is Coral Fellows. She is thirteen, but tells the whisky priest that she rejected God when she was ten. She harbors the priest, an absolute sign of grace to him ("I was hungry and you gave me food; I was thirsty and you gave me drink"; Matt. 25). Spiritually, in spite of her nonbelief, Coral, as the color her name suggests, has the mark of grace, and spiritually she is mature. She is touched deeply by her encounter with the priest, and her intellectual maturity will be reinforced by an understanding of what the priest stands for. Coral's fate is left a mystery, though from the scene that describes the whisky priest's return to the banana station and the Fellowses' conversation at the hotel in the capital one can assume that she met her death either at the hands of Calver or the Red Shirts— another victim of adults.

Greene structured *The Power and the Glory* by design, so that the majority of its sections and subsections are narrated in the third-person-limited point of view of the whisky priest. Yet in spite of the preponderant influence of the priest in the narrative Greene manages to form a masterful representation of the priest's material, as opposed to spiritual, counterpart in the figure of the lieutenant. This is done by a skillful combination of sections focused on the lieutenant himself and those focused on the priest in which the lieutenant figures, so that the reader's composite of him is formed by these two psychological perspectives.

The lieutenant, ideologically, has a good deal in common with Pinkie Brown of *Brighton Rock* and reveals also a touch of Ida Arnold, with both his love of the world and his fuzzy belief in material progress for the Mexican people, which is posed against a strangely demonic-spiritual, indeed priestly quality. He is "a little dapper figure of hate carrying his secret of love."[8] He is described frequently in terms of power and discipline, terms one associates with Pinkie: the scar on the jaw; the revulsion to sex (he is celibate); his ascetic way of life generally; his hatreds, especially for the whisky priest, whom he sees as an enemy who if not exterminated will almost certainly claim him for salvation, a hatred so powerful that it exceeds that of Pinkie's preserved in the phonograph record he cuts for Rose. Like Pinkie he is prepared to "make a massacre" (65). He is as much pursued by the hound of heaven, the traditional metaphor used in Catholic literature to figure

UNDERSTANDING GRAHAM GREENE

God's pursuit of every soul that resists salvation, as the whisky priest is pursued by him, as Pinkie was by Rose.

On three different occasions the lieutenant is in the presence of the whisky priest, twice without knowing it, the last time to arrest him. Ironically, on both earlier occasions he fails to recognize the priest even though certain signs are there. Instead the lieutenant depends on an old photo that shows a plump, well-fed priest in his youth; in the intervening years alcoholism and privation have caused the whisky priest not to resemble the photo at all. On the first occasion, in Maria's village, Brigitta points him out to the lieutenant as her father, which the lieutenant takes as proof positive that he is not the priest. On the second occasion, in prison, the lieutenant performs a work of mercy not only in freeing him but by giving him five pesos, the price of a mass ("I was in prison and you visited me," preaches Christ). On the third occasion the lieutenant goes to the fallen priest Padre José to arrange confession for the whisky priest, an act of charity and treason, and is repelled by the shameful cowardice of the ex-priest who, in spite of the protection of the law, refuses to hear the whisky priest's confession.

Actually there is little need for Padre José's services, for in fact in the preceding scenes the lieutenant has served in the place of a confessor to the whisky priest, in his interrogations, in which not only does the priest confess his shortcomings but witnesses his faith. And in spite of the lieutenant's determination to reject the whisky priest's faith, the whisky priest is convinced that the lieutenant is fundamentally good because of his acts of charity: "I felt at once that you were a good man when you gave me money at the prison" (232); "You're a good man. You've got nothing to be afraid of" (248). For the lieutenant, after the capture of the whisky priest, his life is really over; now that he has caught his quarry, there is nothing left. What the lieutenant's ultimate fate will be is not known. One may surmise even if one cannot know it that it is the lieutenant whom Tench sees officiating at the whisky priest's execution and that he is the officer who, after the firing squad have done their work, administers the coup de grace with his pistol. The whisky priest goes to his death in a shambling manner, frightened but perhaps in the hope that the hound of heaven will hunt down the lieutenant in the end.[9] In such a way will the life of the spirit win over the world, and the lieutenant, not really a person of the world but a true sinner and hater of the world, will in the end be saved, for "the world's unhappy whether you are rich or poor," the priest believes and tells him (233).

The whisky priest, however, is the real concern of this story. Greene has created a modern saint's life that derives from earlier tradition but contributes its own vision of what sainthood should be. The movement in the novel in terms of the whisky priest is quite static, as Greene himself remarked in his interview with Marie-Françoise Allain. Its aim is not to show any change or growth in the priest so much as it is to reveal the totality of his saintliness, which embraces both his virtues and his failings, much as Edmund Spenser figures sainthood, or holiness, in the Redcrosse Knight of book 1 of *The Faerie Queene*, who constantly fails but who has the capacity to persevere in his vocation.

Structurally the novel is built around two elements: first, the framing of the whisky priest's experiences by the perspectives of several other persons in the opening and closing sections of the novel and within that frame the two central sections which focus on the whisky priest; second, the motif of the journey, both literal and spiritual. Parts I and IV, the opening and closing sections, shift almost frantically among Tench, the lieutenant, the Mexican family, Padre José, and Carol, the effect of which is to prepare the reader for the compactness of the narrative of Parts II and III, where the reader is tied closely to the whisky priest. At the same time the narrative moves inexorably toward the convergence of the whisky priest and the lieutenant, who come together, after two earlier meetings, for the last time when the priest is arrested.

The actual movement of the whisky priest can be described as first a linear then a circular journey, beginning in the port town of Frontera and moving to the banana station, to Maria's village, to La Candellaria, to the capital (Villahermosa), where the priest is taken prisoner for violating the temperance law. He is then released, returns to the banana station, thence to the

RELIGION AND THE NOVEL

Indian burial ground, then safely into the state of Chiapas and the Lehrs' *finca*, from which he is called back into Tabasco to minister to the dying Calver, where he is arrested and returned once again to the capital for execution. The capital and death inevitably pull him back to affirm his destiny, which is to die. He is a type not only of Christ but of the prophet Jonah, who in spite of everything he does is called to do God's work, and the whisky priest's geographical itinerary stresses that point.

The whisky priest's spiritual journey is naturally more complex. It consists of his ministry to his people, beginning with his journey with the boy to minister to the boy's mother and ending with his ministry to the lieutenant. It includes an array of humanity, from the hardened criminal Calver to the pious Lehrs, to the Indian mother whose child has been killed, to the mestizo, the Judas who betrays him to the Red Shirts in the end. It reaches its high point in at least three events: in the meeting with Coral Fellows, in the prison scene, and in the dialogue with the lieutenant.

In many ways the prison scene marks the apex of the whisky priest's ministry. It surrounds him with the downtrodden, the forgotten, in all their humanity. He speaks with the pious Catholic woman in the midst of the stench of urine, feces, filthy bodies, and the noises of the body: the wails of suffering, cries of enjoyment rising from the sexual coupling occurring in the darkness of the cell. What Greene has succeeded in doing is to create a microcosm both in the prison scene and in the whisky priest's ministry generally of the Mexican experience and to show that the only true salvation consists in living the gospel message, not in providing only material well-being but in honoring the Christian ideal, which is to show in external acts a goodness to others. Greene's theology is one of works: we are what we do to and for others. There is a grace that operates through the novel among those who feed, shelter, and otherwise minister to the whisky priest. It touches Coral, the villagers, Miss Lehr and, of course, the lieutenant, among others. The operative term is *good,* as Rose in *Brighton Rock* continually tells Pinkie that he is "good" to her, as the whisky priest judges those who minister to him in the spirit of the words of Jesus in Matthew 25:40, "In so far as you did this to one of the least of these brothers of mine, you did it to me." It is the half-caste, the chief of police, the pistoleros, Padre José, all those who live in the world locked in themselves with no sense of "other" who are lost.

Out of this experience Greene creates a saint's life that stresses not personal pride, a greedy hungering after goodness, but rather the signs of grace, a true humanness in the whisky priest in his shabbiness, his alcoholism, his fornication. He fumbles along the path of sainthood not wanting it but, as Greene shows, directed by a providence that surely will not allow him to avoid it. And yet, in spite of his seeming inability to control the larger events, Greene gives him the necessary freedom to feel love and compassion and to serve people in the spirit of his ministry. Though the whisky priest embraces a powerful eschatological view of the world, he does not act out a pious Christianity focused only on personal salvation. He practices a faith very much in the spirit of liberation theology, compatible with a radical socialism that does not reject Christianity. Where he and the lieutenant differ is only in the lieutenant's hatred of all things religious. Otherwise they are doubles.

In spite of Greene's sense of social activism in *The Power and the Glory* many readers are uncomfortable with this novel and are put off by its otherworldly stance that stands in danger of perpetuating the Catholic Church's historical practice of siding with the rich and the powerful and preaching to the masses a palliating Christianity—in Karl Marx's words, a religion that is an opium of the people. Greene's later novels, however, move further in the direction of social activism and further from a preoccupation with issues of faith. No matter what one's judgment of the novel may be, there is no denying that *The Power and the Glory* is one of Greene's most impressive novels on this theme, to be ranked with George Bernanos's *Diary of a Country Priest* and Ignazio Silone's *Bread and Wine*.

UNDERSTANDING GRAHAM GREENE

The Heart of the Matter

Greene's writing career was disrupted somewhat by the war. In spite of his service as an air-raid warden during the blitz and his work in MI6, which occupied him from 1940 to 1944, he did manage to complete one of his best entertainments, *The Ministry of Fear* (1943), which was based in part on his experiences in the blitz. For three years of his service in MI6, in 1942 and 1943, he was posted to Freetown, Sierra Leone, to keep an eye on the Vichy French nearby. It was in a way a home-coming, since Greene and his cousin Barbara had visited the west coast of Africa in 1935, and Greene had written his travel narrative *Journey Without Maps* about their experiences in Liberia. As he had drawn upon his trip to Mexico in *The Power and the Glory*, Greene used his Freetown experience to write what was to be critically and financially his most successful book, *The Heart of the Matter*, published in 1948.[10] Particularly as a Catholic novel *The Heart of the Matter* created a storm of criticism. It also assured Greene's reputation as a major writer and revived interest in his earlier novels, especially *The Power and the Glory*, which, coming as it did at the opening of the war, received little notice and sold poorly.

The Heart of the Matter covers several months of the life of a forty-nine-year-old assistant commissioner of police caught in a crisis of faith brought on by a hollow marriage and a love affair. His character has several antecedents, not the least of whom is the assistant commissioner of *It's a Battlefield*, in whom Greene had prefigured issues of truth, reality, and duty that beset this assistant commissioner, Major Henry Scobie, as well. To his earlier portrait of the public official just returned from duties in the colonies Greene adds a personal dimension to his new assistant commissioner in a way never before done in his fiction.

Up to this point Greene's novels had been largely fabular, strongly allegorical, in the sense that while he may have been drawing on personal experiences, he had never drawn on his personal life to the extent he seems to have done in *The Heart of the Matter*.[11] Scobie's experiences are rooted in the real, psychological, palpable world of everyday life. Greene's current dislike of the book, which he has remarked on variously, seems almost to be a judgment of aspects of his own life he would prefer to forget.[12] In other words Scobie, more than any other character to date, shares an identity with his author. Greene draws one to that observation in his remarks in the introduction to the Collected Edition of the novel: "Scobie was based on nothing but my unconscious."[13] He comments that during its writing "the booby traps I had heedlessly planted in my personal life were blowing up in turn. I had always thought that war would bring death as a solution in one form or another . . . but here I was alive, the carrier of unhappiness to people I loved. . . . So perhaps what I really dislike in the book is the memory of personal anguish" (xii). What

UNDERSTANDING GRAHAM GREENE

in Greene's personal life may link him to this novel must await the biographer's inevitable probing. The point, however, is that *The Heart of the Matter* is an intensely personal novel and shows both faults and virtues arising from that circumstance.

As with his other novels Greene has given this one an "interpretive" title. It is taken from one of Scobie's internal monologues and reflects his desire to understand fully the complexities of existence: "If one knew, he wondered, the facts, would one have to feel pity even for the planets? if one reached what they called the heart of the matter?" (139). The "heart of the matter" is fundamentally the totality of vision that rests with an omniscient God that can account for the problem of evil, natural and moral, and how one is to reconcile it to one's belief in that loving God. Natural evil arises out of circumstances over which human beings have no control. It figures in the deaths of the two children, that of Catherine Scobie and the child who survives the shipwreck. Moral evil arises from human action; it occupies center stage in *The Heart of the Matter*. Against the larger evil of the catastrophes of war—the shipwreck, for example, that Helen Rolt survives—and the machinations of Yusef and the marketeers, Scobie rivets one's attention on the suffering and misfortune he brings to his own life in his effort to hold together a tattered piece of a marriage and carry on an affair with a woman thirty years younger than he. The heart of the matter is to understand fully why this suffering and agony occur,

why, in spite of himself, Scobie acts in ways that can
only cause immense pain; why this must be.

The structure of *The Heart of the Matter* is similar to
that of an Elizabethan tragedy. Unlike Greene's earlier
novels, which structure themselves around a pursuit,
this novel focuses on one character almost to the neglect
of the others, and casts that character's fate in terms
similar to those of a conventional Aristotelian tragic hero:
that of a man better than most, preeminently just, who
through some error of judgment or miscalculation contributes to but is not wholly responsible for his own
ruin. Although Greene maintains that Scobie was solely
the product of his subconscious, it is quite apparent
that he has his literary antecedents, including Hamlet,
with whom he shares that quality of thinking too precisely on the event. The commissioner refers to him as
"Scobie the Just" and affiliates him with Aristides, a
venerated figure from early Greek history (9). Others
in the novel frequently comment on his goodness.

The fall of Scobie can be understood by observing
that structurally the novel has the conventional dramatic
elements of exposition, inciting incident, rising action,
climax, falling action, and catastrophe. It also has the
basic elements of the double plot: what can be called the
public story, or the downfall of Scobie the public official,
ending in the death of Ali, and the private story, of
Scobie's marriage and affair, ending in his suicide. In
the public story Scobie's disintegration can be followed
through from his protection of the captain of the *Esper-*

ance, to borrowing money from Yusef, to being duped in the parrot scheme, to delivering the diamonds to the captain, to Ali's murder. The private story is almost totally internalized in the progression of Scobie's feelings of pity and despair, but in its few outward manifestations it is marked by the departure of Louise for South Africa, the arrival of Helen and the development of Scobie's affair with her, then the return of Louise and the resulting complications, and finally the suicide.

Crucial to the texture of the novel is an awareness of the tensions that exist between the English colonials trying to keep alive the idea of England in a foreign field and the land they find themselves occupying. The English society who occupy Freetown are insular, snobbish, racist. They complain of the weather; they take refuge every evening in their club; they dress for dinner so as to keep their hold on English customs. Out of sheer boredom Harris and Wilson pursue a new sport in the grand English country-life tradition of fox hunting: cockroach hunting. Wilson's proposed membership in the club creates a minor incident, but later he is accepted when it becomes known that he attended a respectable public school. Scobie overhears his wife described snidely as "Literary Louise," and it infuriates him. Harris's racism is evident in his comment on Louise to Wilson, in the first few pages of the novel: "Perhaps if I had a wife like that, I'd sleep with niggers too" (5).

These colonials are much out of their element, as

RELIGION AND THE NOVEL

is revealed in the public story. *The Heart of the Matter* anticipates the treatment of the later political novels, where Greene expounds on the theme of the Old and New Worlds versus the Third World. Anticipating the public disaster is the suicide in the provincial town of Bamba of the district commissioner, young Dickie Pemberton. The interconnection of Pemberton and Scobie is noted by Scobie himself in Louise's nickname for him (Ticki) and its similarity to Dickie. Sierra Leone and its attendant bafflements have proved too much for Pemberton, and he kills himself out of shame over his financial ruin at the hands of a local store manager who is in the employ of the Syrian entrepreneur Yusef. Pemberton exhibits a familiar pattern: misplaced values and a rigid sense of honor, which culminate in a senseless death.

In the "public plot" Scobie the official comes as close as anyone in the British community to understanding the native ways and feeling at home in this place that has been his home for the past fifteen years. His duties in Sierra Leone are to keep the peace and to prevent valuable war materiel from falling into the wrong hands. His actions as an official show him to be a man of compassion but woefully imprudent, yet unafraid to put his career in danger at the hands of the captain of the ship *Esperance* by covering up the captain's indiscreet secreting of a letter and later by personally delivering Yusef's package of diamonds to him. The captain recognizes the extent of Scobie's trust and is overwhelmed by its spirit of goodness. Nevertheless, it is an early sign of Scobie's weakness.

More dangerous, however, and of a different disposition is the Syrian Muslim Yusef, who begins to take Scobie into his control with the loan of the £200 he needs to send Louise out of the country to South Africa. Although Yusef expresses a reverence for Scobie, he also understands power and is not to be trusted under any circumstances. When he comes into possession of Scobie's letter to Helen, no amount of regard can keep him from exploiting his advantage. It is as natural an action to him as breathing. He may admire Scobie's goodness, but he also knows that such a virtue can only be dangerous in a world where so much evil exists. Yusef uses Scobie in a futile effort to do in his rival Tallit, and again, under threat of blackmail, to deliver the package of diamonds, which one can only assume will in the hands of the wrong power contribute ultimately to the deaths of thousands of people.[14] Finally he is instrumental in arranging the murder of Scobie's boy Ali.

When Greene remarked in his interview with Marie-Françoise Allain that the essential concern of all his fiction is with rootlessness, he must have had Scobie in mind, for no matter how much a part of Africa Scobie may think he is, he is essentially a man without roots. His special gifts permit him to be the most expert of the colonials in surviving among and understanding the Africans, but it is not a license of total awareness. When he is on duty that one dark night and unwittingly opens the stench bottle, he is not just the butt of a practical joke; he is the exemplar of Western ignorance and holds himself up to ridicule before the natives. His responsibility for Ali's death rests heavily on his conscience for his failure of trust, his blindness to what is occurring before his eyes. Like Shakespeare's Othello, whom Yusef evokes in a poignant moment in the novel, Scobie is naïve in the ways of this world. He throws away a pearl of great price, his one devoted companion.

As further evidence of his rootlessness, of all Greene's protagonists Scobie has the haziest sense of a past. Although he must possess a past of some significance, he deliberately refuses to call it up into his consciousness and hence deprives readers of access to it. Events from the period prior to his service in Freetown are almost nonexistent. He mentions having played Hotspur in a production of Shakespeare's *Henry IV*, *Part I* at school. Readers know he has been in Freetown for the past fifteen years. But what do they know of the previous thirty-four years? Almost nothing. Scobie moves in an eternal present, with two systems to ballast him: his ethical code as an official of the British government and his Catholicism.

Greene has remarked that "the character of Scobie was intended to show that pity can be the expression of an almost monstrous pride" (xiv). In his failed marriage and his aborted affair Scobie seems almost by an act of will to want to take to himself all the burdens and miseries of the world, but particularly the unhappiness of Louise and Helen, for whose misery he assumes himself to be the cause. Neither is particularly likable. Greene attributes Louise's stiffness to the technical problem of projecting her character through the personality of Scobie and to a lesser extent through Wilson. Yet beyond her lack of sentimentality she is personally and spiritually cold, and reveals a touch of evil in the way she torments Scobie after her return from the South African stay, by forcing him to mass after mass to further damn himself by taking Communion in a state of mortal sin. At the same time her abuse of Wilson is amply justified. Her realism balances Scobie's sentimentalism, but she still has that quality of bitchiness that makes one feel that Greene himself disliked her too much to be able to construct any part of the novel around her consciousness.

Helen Rolt suffers from a lack of credibility. No matter how much a nineteen-year-old might mature through a forty-day horror and an early widowhood, she remains too savvy for her age. Like Carol Fellows in *The Power and the Glory* she is an agnostic; she has rebelled against her clergyman's-daughter upbringing. Her iconoclastic reactions to Scobie's heartfelt but constricting Catholicism are also welcome counterpoints. In her own way she is the true survivor, the one who carries on, endures, like Rose in *Brighton Rock* and Kate Farrant in *England Made Me*. It is not difficult to understand why Scobie falls in love with her. She is both

RELIGION AND THE NOVEL

daughter and lover, the daughter who died, the wife he never had, but she can understand the limit of her demand on him and is rightly critical of his inability to separate her unhappiness from his. In the revealing letter Scobie leaves her, which falls into Yusef's hands, Scobie says, *"I love you more than myself, more than my wife, more than God I think"* (209). This is a shocking statement, surely the misplaced devotion of a man who has lost all sense of self-worth and stands in danger of yielding to despair.

To Scobie's Shakespearean tragic models can be added Christopher Marlowe's Dr. Faustus, whose predicament in that play is similar in certain ways to Scobie's. Marlowe has given a powerful representation of a man who creates his own hell. Faustus's tempter Mephistophilis says that "this [the world] is hell, nor am I out of it" (I.iv.80).[15] In a similar way, not through the cultivation of an unbridled hedonism but through a brooding self-inflicted torture, Scobie creates for himself a living hell from which death is an escape, a way out, even preferable to life. He exhibits an overbearing pride that expresses itself in both his belief that all human happiness is dependent on him and that he must carry the burden of pity for the miseries of others. Even God himself will be at peace, once rid of Henry Scobie. In his final dialogue with the voice of God, in which he almost can hear the sacrament lodged within him speak to him, Scobie echoes Faustus's last agonizing soliloquy. In spite of his knowledge that forgiveness is near, Scobie cannot break through to it. "It's not repentance you [Scobie] lack, it's just a few simple actions: to go up to the Nissen hut and say good-bye. Or if you must, continue rejecting me but without lies anymore," says the God within him, but like Faustus he cannot believe that such a burden can be shifted so easily from himself to God (305).

The nearer literary ancestor of Scobie, however, is Captain Edward Ashburnham of Ford Madox Ford's *The Good Soldier*, a writer Greene admires deeply, and whom Greene edited for the Bodley Head.[16] About Ford's art Greene says that no writer in this century except James has been as skilled a craftsman, and he considers *The Good Soldier* to be Ford's finest book.[17] A knowledge of the basic lines of the novel is instructive in understanding *The Heart of the Matter*. The story of *The Good Soldier* is narrated by an American, John Dowell, a well-meaning but at times psychically blind narrator, and concerns an English military officer who has made a bad marriage to a devout Anglo-Irish Catholic girl, Leonora. In spite of his efforts to maintain the highest code of conduct, Captain Ashburnham carries on affairs, accumulates devastating gambling debts from which his wife continually rescues him, and finally brings his tragic life to a crisis by falling in love with his ward, a lovely teen-age girl named Nancy Rufford. This final quasi-incestuous disaster prompts him to take the only way out of the situation he knows, and he kills himself. His wife remarries after his death, has a family, and lives quite happily.

RELIGION AND THE NOVEL

Ford's memorable opening line of *The Good Soldier* might well be applied to *The Heart of the Matter:* "This is the saddest story I have ever heard." The parallels between the two love triangles are apparent, as it is obvious that Greene found the germ of his African story in Ford's novel. Leonora, Nancy, and Captain Ashburnham stand in relation to each other as do Louise, Helen Rolt, and Major Scobie. Louise's pietism and rigid Catholicism are like those of Leonora Ashburnham. The connection between Helen Rolt and Nancy Rufford is more tenuous but a firm one nonetheless.

The illuminating parallels occur, of course, between Edward Ashburnham and Henry Scobie. Edward is known to readers, as are all the characters in Ford's novel, through the narrator Dowell, who tries in his fallible way by misdirection and indirection to help them understand this honorable man driven by a forbidden passion he cannot control, that scorches his very soul and ultimately drives him to suicide. Scobie is known more directly through Greene's use of third-person-limited point of view. Ashburnham is not driven by a profound faith but rather by a desire to maintain the code of the gentleman and an outward show of respect for the rigid Catholicism of his wife. This he finds he cannot do without overwhelming torment, and so kills himself to resolve his dilemma and to free both women from his shameful passion.

Scobie's plight, so frequently analyzed in theological terms, is that of postmodern man, who wanders not between two worlds, one dead, the other powerless to be born, in Matthew Arnold's words, but rather posits existentially the world of values he inhabits. For Scobie that world lies in the certitude provided by the Catholic faith he has adopted as a convert. Scobie is a man without a country, without a culture, without, most significantly, a philosophical and intellectual framework. Of all Greene's characters who pretend to some social and cultural standing he is the least intellectual.[18] He rarely reads books, owns almost none, dislikes poetry or any literature that reveals human feeling. Early in the novel Greene describes him as a man who constructs his living space, and one might add his view of the world, through a systematic process of reduction, of shedding. In an effort to overcome that rootlessness of which Greene has spoken, Scobie finds structure in the teaching of the Church. He feels no commitment to the traditions that the English community cling to so pathetically in *The Heart of the Matter*. His allegiance to the professional code erodes in the course of the novel. He turns to the rigid logic of his faith, which presents him with an inflexible moral code that pushes him to extremes of guilt and pity, and inevitably fails him.

His flaw is his inability to realize a concept of self out of the cultural and personal wasteland he inhabits, and thus is tortured by the fiery cloak of his Catholicism, from which suicide comes as a release from suffering. It is interesting to notice how Scobie's ultimate destiny is of much less importance than is Pinkie's and

RELIGION AND THE NOVEL

that Greene's obligatory epilogue (a survivor consults a priest) in *The Heart of the Matter* has Father Rank almost portraying the judgment of Scobie as an irrelevancy. The net effect is to make this seemingly most religious of Greene's novels to be far more concerned with the secular. The real concern of the novel, and novels that come after it, is with the failure of a stultified faith to minister to the needs of a new age and to overcome the disillusionment that awaits those who believe they can cope with the world through it. Scobie does fail, true, but in many ways the faith he turned to, as he understood that faith, failed him. He would have been far more able to survive with either Louise's simplistic piety and certitude or Helen's agnosticism, if he had been capable of making those choices. One can only wish for this tortured man the realization beyond death of his dream in which he and Ali are walking through "a wide cool meadow" with birds overhead, where, when he reclines on the grass, a small green snake slithers harmlessly over his arm and touches "his cheek with a cold, friendly, remote tongue" (91).[19]

The End of the Affair

Following the publication of *The Heart of the Matter* by some three years, Greene's next religious novel represents both a deepening of the religious theme in his work and a revolution in his narrative technique. *The End of the Affair* is a haunting novel in its development of a variation on the predicament of Scobie in *The Heart of the Matter;* in this novel Sarah Miles stands in relation to her husband, Henry, and her lover, Maurice Bendrix, as Scobie does to Louise and Helen Rolt.[20] As a novel of religious struggle *The End of the Affair* is subtler, however, and more natural and sympathetic in its treatment of its religious theme.

For many years Greene had continued to follow the process of developing his narrative structures through the indirection provided by the use of a blend of third-person-limited point of view and an intermittent, punctuating authorial voice that shifts from character to character, providing in the totality of the narrative pieces of a puzzle that the reader can fit into a coherent whole. At the same time, in various stories written and published through 1940 Greene had made some apprenticing moves in the direction of the use of first-person point of view.[21] These early exercises are limited to fairly straightforward narrators who tend not to put a personal stamp on the stories they tell. The commitment to a more sustained effort using this technique did not occur until later, in his development of a film script for *The Third Man,* in which he chose to have the story narrated by Calloway, a British army officer.

Inspired by a rereading of Dickens's *Great Expectations* and impressed continually by the artistry of Ford's *The Good Soldier,* and especially by what Ford could achieve

through the voice of Dowell, Greene set about imitating
and exploiting the subtleties Ford was able to generate
in his book, subtle enough to be described by one critic
as "the finest French novel in the English language."[22]
It was a difficult apprenticeship: "Many a time I regret-
ted pursuing 'I' along his dismal road and contemplated
beginning *The End of the Affair* all over again with Bendrix
seen from outside in the third person."[23] Nevertheless,
out of this effort came Maurice Bendrix, author and narrator, partaking to a great degree in Greene's own habits
as a writer, and the moving story of the end of his affair
with Sarah Miles, the unhappy wife of a successful but
emotionally inhibited civil servant.

This briefest of Greene's novels is also structurally
its most complex, employing as it does a narrator who,
while not so fallible as Ford's John Dowell, is still very
much involved in telling his story as he understands it.
Of course, unlike Dowell, he has the advantage of being
a novelist himself.

To better understand the frame of the novel it may
be helpful to recast that frame in terms of its chronol-
ogy. Bendrix is situated in time in 1949, narrating a
series of events covering mainly a period from the summer of 1939, when his affair with Sarah began, to her
death in late February 1946. Following the sequence of
events at times becomes confusing, but expert readers
familiar with either *The Good Soldier* or Faulkner's *The
Sound and the Fury* will accustom themselves readily to
Bendrix's strategies. From a three-year distance Bendrix

picks up the thread of events in a brief period of a little more than a month, from January 10, 1946, when Henry Miles seeks his assistance in uncovering Sarah's secret life, to some time in late February of 1946, after her death.[24] Within that frame Bendrix recollects his affair with her, extending from the summer of 1939 to June 16, 1944, and the V-1 bomb attack, in which he is thought to have died and when Sarah prays to God to bring Bendrix back to life. Some minimal coverage of earlier events is also included. Readers know that Sarah was probably born about 1908—she is mentioned as being around thirty-eight years of age in 1946—and that she was baptized in France at the age of two, or about 1910. It is known, too, that she was married in 1929, presumably at about age twenty-one.

Bendrix's strategy is to eschew the artistry of the storyteller, which he is by profession, and follow the track of his feelings, with narrative, reminiscence, and excerpts from Sarah's journal mixed together. He says pointedly at one juncture that if this were a novel, he would end it then and there. The device of Sarah's journal of course allows Greene to develop her own voice, though at several points in it Greene clearly would prefer to have her write her own novel, dialogue and all, rather than allow her to be the reflective chronicler she ought always to be. By this fairly complex process readers are allowed gradually to pull the story together and by indirections find directions out.

The title of the novel refers literally to the end of

RELIGION AND THE NOVEL

the affair between Sarah and Bendrix on that tragic day in 1944, but the "affair" is not only their love affair. It is also the story of the close of Sarah's life. It is, most importantly, the end of the earthly stage of her affair with God, as she moves spiritually through a wasteland marked by dead and dying relationships closer and closer to a belief in and acceptance of and love for God. Greene took as his inspiration for the novel, which came to him on the isle of Capri in December 1948, Friedrich von Hügel's life of St. Catherine of Genoa, a saint who devoted herself to attending the sick during two major outbreaks of the bubonic plague. St. Catherine and her husband, Giuliano Adorno, lived out the later years of their marriage in continence, and both devoted themselves to good works. Sarah is a modern type of St. Catherine, moving in her own way through London, searching for God, performing tender acts of love, and touching in her special way the lives of those around her.

Bendrix sets out to narrate the actions leading to the end of the one affair, but it is really the other affair that becomes the subject of his story. This affair draws its inspiration from a passage from another work by von Hügel, which is at the core of this novel. Greene quotes the passage in his introduction to the Collected Edition of the novel: "The purification and slow constitution of the Individual into a Person, by means of the Thing-element, the apparently blind Determinism of Natural Law and Natural Happenings. . . . Nothing can be more certain than that we must admit and place this undeniable, increasingly obtrusive, element and power *somewhere* in our lives: if we will not own it as a means, it will grip us as our end."

The End of the Affair consummates the direction of Greene's religious development as a novelist; it presents the reader with both a character and perspective that represent an advance in technique and in philosophy over the novels that preceded it. Sarah Miles is a modern saint, in the sense that she exhibits the true marks of sainthood, and through her Greene constructs within the context of the Western experience the qualities of sainthood that are reflected in the Third World of *The Power and the Glory*. With the whisky priest she shares that sense of destiny that marked him; with Pinkie she shares his *accidia*, his weariness of the world; and with Scobie, his need to bring love into the lives of others.

What distinguishes her from the others is her power to heal in both a spiritual and material sense, as is revealed in the special grace that marks her—from her secret baptism, to her intercession to save Bendrix, her healing of Lance Parkis, and her effect on Richard Smythe's blemish.[25] All these events Greene intended to have a natural explanation; but they are also intended through their cumulative effect to have an impact on Bendrix, not Sarah, whose existence is in a state of dramatic crisis, and it is through Bendrix's consciousness that one is led to a full appreciation of her true nature.

As Bendrix unfolds the tale, Sarah proceeds through

RELIGION AND THE NOVEL

stages of development, moving from a stereotypical un-fulfilled housewife to a holy person. It is important to understand the latter state in its full meaning so that piety not be confused with holiness. Piety is a pharisai-cal pursuit of religion concentrated on the selfish devel-opment of religious virtue independent of the world and of sinfulness. It is the rigid faith of the Lehrs in *The Power and the Glory*. Holiness, on the other hand, is a virtue related to its association with "wholeness," with the totality of the person, with the struggle that occurs as the person deals with the world. What is represented in Sarah is the movement, as von Hügel describes it in the passage quoted by Greene, from individualism to personhood.

Bendrix serves as the consciousness through which Sarah's goodness is fully revealed, and in that regard he is a figure also consciously ironic, because he realizes that in his need to tell his story he is witness to her biography of faith and is an advocate of her goodness. Bendrix the agnostic, egoist, and materialist is forced to behold through its gradual unfolding the full blossom-ing of Sarah's personhood. Bendrix achieves this end by participating in a traditional Greene pursuit. At the opening of the novel Bendrix describes how he was ap-proached by Henry Miles and asked to find out whether Sarah is having an affair, and though Henry changes his mind, Bendrix engages Parkis to follow Sarah. Bendrix's discovery is, of course, that her "affair" is with God. The discovery proceeds through stages of revelation, beginning with her characterization in books 1 and 2 as a desperately unhappy and unfaithful married woman, victimized by both husband and lover. Book 3, which consists of Bendrix's reading in her stolen journal, opens up a deeper awareness of her growing religious faith. Book 4 provides a touching, painful view of Sarah's agony during her last days.

Book 5, with its delayed exposition of Sarah's childhood through her mother's confidences and Bendrix's browsing in Sarah's books, gives the fullest dimension of her sense of selflessness and her true feeling for others. In Bendrix, Greene has developed a largely credible voice, modern in its assertion of self, in its hatred of anything "miraculous" or "magical," in its rages of jealousy, especially of God himself, whose existence and power Bendrix affirms in the very act of hating. From a perspective of three years, in which he has had time to ponder the meaning of Sarah's life and her effects in the changes her presence wrought, Bendrix admits that what began as a chronicle of hate has turned out badly: "Perhaps my hatred is really as deficient as my love" (58).

Greene's portrayal of Sarah is a subtle blend of and answer to the complications afforded in the religious crises of his earlier protagonists. It is with regard to Scobie, however, that Sarah's experience is most enlightening. Like Scobie she is caught in a love triangle, but unlike him she does not suffer agonies of guilt, because she has come to terms with her life in a way that

RELIGION AND THE NOVEL

Scobie, with his self-condemnation, could not. Sarah's quasi-Catholic condition allows her the freedom to be unfailingly herself and to express herself in terms that are more humane and personal than those of Scobie's adopted faith. He is trapped, like Bendrix, in egoism, dominance, personal guilt, while she is free to move to a higher level. To a certain extent Scobie is a victim of his gender, which is the wellspring of his pride. It requires that he not only be resolved of all doubt as to his responsibilities but that he also behave in a chivalrous manner; while Sarah, who sees and understands the needs of her men, who fall quite below her in stature, is able to endure the pain of loss without magnifying the guilt beyond all sensible understanding.

The question of Sarah's miraculous gifts vexes many readers. Her gifts, however, are part of the mystery of a world that is just as puzzling in its seeming contradiction of the rules of nature as in God's mercy in *Brighton Rock*. One cannot have a religious world without divine immanence to remind one of the presence of this quality of one's life. More than even the whisky priest, Sarah Miles is touched by the divine both in her nature and in her effect on the world. Greene sees her as specially marked in her baptism, her selflessness, and her ability to change the world both physically through her power and spiritually through her example. She is the last of his good and saved characters; none are to follow her in the books to come.

UNDERSTANDING GRAHAM GREENE

A Burnt-out Case

The End of the Affair marks the end of Greene's affair with the religious novel after a successful exploration of its themes and motifs from 1938 to 1951. Without taking anything away from the three earlier novels, it is fitting to see *The End of the Affair* as an appropriate close to Greene's exploration of religious themes. Coming after a ten-year hiatus, the one remaining "religious" book, *A Burnt-out Case*, represents a different approach to the religious novel and a different attitude toward religion itself.

The extraordinary popularity of *The Heart of the Matter* and the critical acclaim accorded *The End of the Affair* secured for Greene a reputation as one of the most talented Catholic writers of his time. His subsequent experiences, however, attest to the harsh effect of this unwanted notoriety. Beset by all manner of religious quacks, lost souls in search of Holy Mother Church, and people with genuine needs, Greene, always a reclusive person, after some efforts to provide the spiritual leadership asked of him, drew away from this onslaught of petitioners. His career in the 1950s took him deeper into his earlier calling, journalism, and thrust him into the arena of world politics and the political novel, and he turned only infrequently in the direction of Catholicism and the problems of his faith. What little one finds of religious themes appears in his two plays, *The Living Room* and *The Potting Shed*, discussed below in chapter

RELIGION AND THE NOVEL

6. His interest in fiction turned toward world politics, as figured in his major works from this period, *The Third Man*, *The Quiet American*, and *Our Man in Havana*. He traveled to Malaya, to Indochina, Kenya, Poland, Haiti, Russia, Cuba, and in 1959 to the Congo, in search of both news stories and material for his fiction. This last journey, to visit the leper colony at Yonda, Greene wrote up as his "Congo Journal," published in the collection *In Search of a Character*; it was also the source of material for his last major religious novel, *A Burnt-out Case*.

The title of the novel takes its meaning from a phrase used to describe the condition of lepers, or more properly victims of Hansen's disease, after its ravages have run their course. Its symbolic application is to the protagonist of the novel, Querry the architect, a stateless and placeless figure in the tradition of Scobie, who has himself been ravaged by his self-centeredness, has brought immense suffering to others, lost his faith, and now finds himself spiritually a "burnt-out case."

Of all Greene's books *A Burnt-out Case* is the most lacking in story, the most static, and in many ways the least appealing. As Greene himself describes it, the novel is a kind of allegory of states of belief and unbelief, in which particular characters represent those states: Dr. Colin "a settled and easy atheism," the Superior "a settled and easy belief," Father Thomas "an unsettled form of belief," and "Querry an unsettled form of disbelief." The Congo is both the world of the mind and the world at large, and the leper colony the community of God's sufferers who bear the marks of tragically maimed lives.[26] Much of Querry's story is taken up with the details of leprosy and the lengths to which the victims of that horrible disease go to endure life in the face of such hopelessness. Confronting this challenge, the lepers grow in stature, evolve under the watchful eyes of Dr. Colin, showing by the way how much Greene's view of human nature had been influenced by his careful reading of Teilhard de Chardin's *Phenomenon of Man.*[27] In a sense one can feel in the novel Greene's temptation to pursue their fate at the hands of the comfortable white *colons,* or plantation owners and managers, at war with his commitment to get on with Querry's story. In the end it is the lepers who are the real heroes of the novel, and Querry an incidental figure bridging sympathetically the chasm between the natives and the white community. Greene's purpose, however, prevails in the novel, and he picks up the threads of Querry's search and brings it to its conclusion.

Querry, the disbeliever, is at the center of the story, and yet in his coldness he lacks the vitality that attracts one to his predecessors Scobie and Bendrix. He enters the leprosarium only to escape his past, yet he runs directly into it and stands in danger of having saint-hood, of all things, thrust upon him by Parkinson the journalist and Rycker the palm-oil factory manager. Like Goethe's Faust his wish is, after a life of self-indulgence, to find peace, ideally to locate Pendélé, the nirvana that his African boy Deo Gratias seeks also. Instead he becomes the victim of an absurd and tawdry melodrama, and is killed by the jealous husband Rycker, who thinks Querry is the father of Maria Rycker's unborn child.

The novel, flawed as it is, is perhaps for all that a proper closing to Greene's novels on religious themes. It leaves one with a sense of watching the end of a journey. Querry has passed through phases of belief out the other side into the world of the disbeliever, but out of his commitment he is confounded into acceptance of the truth of God, just as much as Bendrix is in his efforts to deny him. George Herbert, the seventeenth-century poet, describes this state perfectly in his poem "The Pulley":

> Yet let him keep the rest
> But keep them with repining restlesnesse:
> Let him be rich and wearie, that at least,
> If goodness leade him not, yet wearinesse
> May tosse him to my breast.

Querry is such a person, showing that in the very act of caring he exhibits the great faith of one who in the intensity of his disbelief provides affirmation. Once again, in the words Greene quotes from Charles Péguy in the epigraph to *The Heart of the Matter*, no one is as well versed in matters of Christianity as is the sinner, no one, that is, unless he be a saint. In many ways Querry, who has been taken by critics to be Greene's embodiment of the rejection of belief, is of the party of Pinkie, the whisky priest, Scobie, and Bendrix, of that of the Christian *malgré lui*, in spite of himself. One may wish *A Burnt-out Case* to have been a better book, but in his closing out of the theme of faith in his fiction Greene has created someone remarkably like his earlier characters, far less complex and fascinating, but suffering along with them through the challenges of unbelief, disbelief, and belief.

Notes

1. A good historical account of the situation in Tabasco is given in J. W. F. Dulles, *Yesterday in Mexico* (Austin: University of Texas Press, 1961) 611–24.

2. *The Lawless Roads* (London: Heinemann and Bodley Head, 1978) 141.

3. Philip Stratford points out important similarities also between the leper priest Father Damien and the whisky priest, in *Faith and Fiction* (Notre Dame, IN: University of Notre Dame Press, 1964) 29, 218–19.

4. Copies of the photographs were added in the Uniform Edition of *The Lawless Roads* (London: Heinemann, 1955) between pp. 52–53. For a biography of Father Pro see Fanchon Royer, *Padre Pro* (New York: Kennedy, 1954). The photographs, which were intended to instill fear in the populace, had the contrary effect of advancing Pro's martyrdom.

5. Greene contributed an introduction to Fr. Philip Caraman's translation of Gerard's *The Autobiography of an Elizabethan* (London: Longmans, Green, 1951), in which he refers once also to the martyrdom of Pro. Greene mentions the parallel to Elizabeth's persecution in *Ways of Escape* (London: Bodley Head, 1980) 84.

RELIGION AND THE NOVEL

6. Because Phyllis Bentley's historical novel *Take Courage* was being published in 1940 in the United States under the title *The Power and the Glory*, Viking chose as an alternate the less impressive *The Labyrinthine Ways*, taken from Francis Thompson's religious poem "The Hound of Heaven." Later the American title was changed to *The Power and the Glory*.

7. Sean O'Faolain, "Graham Greene: I Suffer; Therefore I Am," *The Vanishing Hero* (London: Eyre and Spottiswoode, 1956) 73–79; George Orwell, "The Sanctified Sinner," *Graham Greene: A Collection of Critical Essays,* ed. Samuel Hynes (Englewood Cliffs, NJ: Prentice-Hall, 1973) 105. Orwell thinks Greene used the religious allegory successfully in *The Power and the Glory* but not in *The Heart of the Matter.*

8. Greene, *The Power and the Glory* (London: Heinemann and Bodley Head, 1971) 66. Further references are to this edition and will be noted parenthetically.

9. Greene's epigraph to this novel, taken from John Dryden's *The Hind and the Panther* (2.5–6), applies to both of them: "Th'inclosure narrow'd; the sagacious power / Of hounds and death drew nearer every hour."

10. Discussions of the text of *The Heart of the Matter* that should be consulted are David Leon Higdon, "Graham Greene's Second Thoughts: The Text of *The Heart of the Matter,*" *Studies in Bibliography* 30 (1977): 249–56, and Philip Stratford, "Second Thoughts on Graham Greene's 'Second Thoughts': The Five Texts of *The heart of the Matter,*" *Studies in Bibliography* 31 (1978): 263–66.

11. R. W. B. Lewis comments on the return to traditional forms in *the Heart of the Matter* in "The Trilogy," *Graham Greene: A Collection of Critical Essays* 69–70.

12. Marie-Françoise Allain, *The Other Man: Conversations with Graham Greene* (New York: Simon and Schuster, 1983) 22.

13. *The Heart of the Matter* (London: Heinemann and Bodley Head, 1971) xv; further references are to this edition and are noted parenthetically.

14. Scobie contemplates the ultimate effect of the diamonds: "In

our hearts there is a ruthless dictator, ready to contemplate the misery of a thousand strangers if it will ensure the happiness of the few we love" (221).

15. Denis Marion suggests that this vision of life as a hell on earth is what is most distinctive about the novel: "Graham Greene," *La table ronde* Feb. 1950: 173–79.

16. *The Bodley Head Ford Madox Ford,* 4 vols. (London: Bodley Head, 1962–63). A helpful survey of Ford's influence on Greene is given in Karen Radell, *Affirmation in a Moral Wasteland* (New York: Peter Lang, 1987).

17. "Ford Madox Ford," *Collected Essays* (New York: Viking, 1969) 161.

18. Joseph Hynes discusses this point in "The 'Facts' at *The Heart of the Matter,*" *Texas Studies in Literature and Language* 13 (1972): 717.

19. This scene calls to mind one in Shakespeare's *As You Like It* (IV.iii.108–13), in which Oliver describes being approached by a green snake while sleeping in the Forest of Arden. That snake, which slithers off into the forest, here is changed to a figure of love, not harm, and nature and Scobie are at one with each other.

20. For a discussion of this substantially revised text see David Leon Higdon, "'Betrayed Intentions': The Text of Graham Greene's *The End of the Affair,*" *Library,* n.s. 6, 1 (1979): 70–77.

21. These stories show Greene's practicing with first person: "The Innocent," "Across the Bridge," "The Hint of an Explanation," "The Second Death," "A Day Saved," "The Case for the Defence," and "Alas, Poor Maling."

22. Mark Shorer quoting John Rodker in his introduction, *The Good Soldier* (New York: Vintage, 1955) vi-vii.

23. Introduction, *The End of the Affair* (London: Heinemann and Bodley Head, 1974) viii.

24. For a detailed analysis of the time-theme structure of the novel see Ronald G. Walker, "World without End: An Approach to Narrative Structure in Greene's *The End of the Affair,*" *Texas Studies in Literature and Language* 26 (1984): 218–41.

RELIGION AND THE NOVEL

25. In the Collected Edition, Greene altered the text to describe Smythe's condition as urticaria, a skin disorder, so as to give it the possibility of a natural explanation. The alteration detracts from the possibilities of the miraculous by assuming that all conditions must subscribe to a definition of "natural" that falls within the bounds of scientific knowledge as we have it at this moment in time, while the earlier condition of the blemish allows for a fuller and more mysterious interpretation; i.e., that miracles are those occurrences that at this moment in time defy scientific explanation, that in the future may or may not allow for such an explanation.

26. Introduction, *A Burnt-out Case* (London: Heinemann and Bodley Head, 1974).

27. Gwen Boardman, *Graham Greene: The Aesthetics of Exploration* (Gainesville: University of Florida Press, 1971) 132.

CHAPTER FOUR

Novels and Politics,
1950–1970

A judgment not original to this study is that Greene's stature as a writer will continue to grow over the next several generations, because his novels have a particular attraction for the English-speaking world beyond the Anglo-American pale and hence outside the often narrowly based concerns of recent Anglo-American fiction.[1] Despite his long-standing devotion to Henry James and the James tradition, Greene's comments sometimes reflect a dissatisfaction with the introspective novel, particularly in his critical remarks on the work of Virginia Woolf, E. M. Forster, and the Bloomsbury group, whom he faults for their lack of engagement with the outer world of human experience—or what can be called here, for want of a better word, the world of politics.[2]

For Greene human action ultimately derives from political relationships and is rooted in those relationships in both an economic and a spiritual sense. In large measure he is a product of England between the wars, of the period of the diminution of the Empire, of the

NOVELS AND POLITICS 1950–1970

Great Depression, the hunger marches, the strikes of the 20s and 30s. His own politics are far from easy to define, but it is clear in all his writing, even in the most religious of his work, that the clash of class, the struggle of have-nots, the deprivation of the Third World—in other words, the concerns of politics—are not far from the crises of faith that his most spiritually afflicted protagonists experience.

This motif can be detected in the novels that have already been discussed in chapters 2 and 3. It has its beginning in Greene's early thriller *Stamboul Train*, where the characters move against a backdrop of political intrigue. In *It's a Battlefield*, which Greene has called his most political novel, the circumstances are the strike and the riots that London experienced during that troubled time, and Conrad Drover's crisis provides a specific instance of the more general political crisis. In *England Made Me* it is the rootlessness of Kate and Tony Farrant, and the greed of Krogh. Although spiritual aridity dominates *Brighton Rock*, an equally important aspect of the novel is the economic deprivation, the sordidness of life in Brighton.

With *The Power and the Glory* Greene moves to a new and enduring principle of development in his work: the juxtaposition of Euro-American traditions and that of the victims of Euro-American enslavement, outside the bounds of England and later the United States. It is impossible not to read *The Power and the Glory* without being deeply moved by the dangers of the benevolent despotism of the lieutenant and the concomitant exploitation of the peasantry by politicians and *colons,* and the clash of those forces with the primitivism of the native populace as it is expressed in their humanity, their social cohesiveness, and their religion. This melding of spiritual and political can be seen as well in the African works, *The Heart of the Matter* and *A Burnt-out Case,* where the benevolence of Westerners is compromised by their contempt for those they seek to lift up. Scobie and Querry are always outsiders, though not exploitative, uncaring people like Rycker in *A Burnt-out Case* or the civil service community in *The Heart of the Matter.*

Often what Greene aims for is a widening of the earlier themes of his mentor Joseph Conrad into a political-fictional form of moral force, in which the allegory of the struggle becomes the focus of each story. In the novel generally any political drama (the term is used here in a general not a generic sense) tends to develop along Marxian lines. It draws its vigor from the conflict between a privileged class and an underclass, specifically between classes within a defined political unit like a country, or between an enslaved underclass in that nation and its master, usually a colonial power exercising hegemony through a puppet government propped up by an elite class of wealthy natives. Of such political experiences in our time one has ample evidence, and Greene's fictions come at a point in history where these struggles have become the paramount concern of world politics.

NOVELS AND POLITICS 1950–1970

Of Greene's politics something more definite should be said. Like many of his generation he had a brief flirtation with communism in the 20s; he was a party member, but only briefly. On the other hand, he has been critical of Labor governments and at one point expressed some mild support for Tory Prime Minister Margaret Thatcher in the first year of her government. Since then, however, he has been critical of her. Being such an anti-ideologue, Greene often can be better defined by what he is against politically. He is opposed to imperialism; he is opposed to totalitarianism. He is for human rights, for the right especially of self-determination for native populations. While highly individual in his beliefs and to many critics disturbingly contradictory, one can say that he is of a leftist bent, Marxist to the extent of any writers of the Left who find their material in the existence of class struggle. Greene tends to avoid the pallid dramas so much admired by the Right, which, like the novels of his fellow writer Evelyn Waugh (and with whom from time to time he has been inappropriately linked by critics), are often vicious critiques of a failed aristocracy or intelligentsia, who have botched badly their obligation to reach out to those less gifted, less fortunate than they. Rather, Greene is the forebear of the new writers who in "doing" the political novel necessarily find their inspiration in the moral issues raised by exploitation and deprivation of human rights. In this country of political morality Greene is well at home; in fact, he is one of the most gifted among Anglo-

American writers and an inspiration to Third World writers working in the English-language tradition, many of whom he has read and encouraged and who look to him as their mentor.

His perspective, however, must necessarily be different from theirs. Where they speak from a native tradition that grows stronger each year, his voice is that of the outsider. He focuses on characters with Western perspectives, who respond to native political crises that they understand somewhat vaguely but who express a large measure of sympathy for the plight of the downtrodden. Greene has been widely received as a writer in the Third World because his novels eschew the subtle patronizing of writers like Forster and Orwell, and also his mentor Conrad, who speaks with the voice of an earlier generation. His best fictional character, perhaps, in that regard is Scobie—intelligent and sympathetic but limited in awareness because he is a foreigner.

Equally appealing to Greene as a persona for his political novels is the secret agent, either as an agent of a foreign government (*The Confidential Agent*), as a spy, (*The Human Factor* and *The Quiet American*), as a spy *manqué* (*Our Man in Havana*), or as a free agent, acting on his own, carrying as it were his own portfolio (*The Third Man*). Among Greene's postwar political novels those dealing with espionage are of special interest because of the focus espionage gives to the ethical issues that the characters must confront, particularly in their efforts to maintain some kind of ethic in the face of powerful technocracies whose only ethic is expediency. Where most spy fiction tends to look at characters superficially as being either patriotically motivated or in the game for the love of the game, Greene probes deeper. His protagonists must confront choices more complex than those found in conventional spy fiction. They resolve their dilemmas by rejecting patriotic cant and romantic escapism and by trying to find some anchor in the people they love, acting out in their own way W. H. Auden's famous dictum, "We must love one another or die."

In contrast to the somewhat bland representations of spying in his prewar novels, his postwar portrayals are sharper because they are infused with a more powerful sense of geopolitical issues. This infusion had three sources: the possibilities created by a new subject matter at the close of World War II, Greene's first having known and visited the places where the later novels were set, and, last, his having been in the Secret Service and seen intelligence activity close up. This last confirms a truth often noted about Greene: that his best work seems always to grow out of his personal experiences. What did he gain from these experiences that he could use in his writing? First, a sharper sense of the tawdriness and boredom that comprises most of the business of spying. Secondly, the belief that individual worth and individual ethics outweigh the claims of national security and the need to protect the state.

The Third Man

With his extensive knowledge of and experience with the medium of film, and the distinctive mark that the genre had put on his fiction, it seemed perhaps only a matter of time before that experience would bear fruit, which it did in his novel/film *The Third Man*, which has become a classic. Greene describes his work on the film with director Carol Reed in his introduction to the Collected Edition of the novel. As he has noted in several places, *The Third Man* was in its conception and execution a film, and the prefilm "novelization" or "treatment" existed only as a means to that end. It is clear, however, that both have their special force, for the mark of the skilled novelist is all too evident in the deft handling of the printed version. What it may lack in sophisticated use of point of view it makes up for in the texture of Greene's descriptions, which do not always translate sufficiently into film. *The Third Man* has contributed both an epithet and an atmosphere that have become distinctive marks of Cold War fiction. The phrase "the third man" has become part of the language of espionage. The atmosphere of the novel, that of postwar Vienna divided into sections controlled by each of the four powers, is a microcosm of the Cold War world with its two competing authorities, the Allied Powers and the Soviets.

Its main character, Harry Lime, is Greene's most famous Doppelgänger. He is a mysterious figure, a gentleman with an enviable public school and university education. His name Greene chose to signify the quick-lime used to hasten the decomposition of corpses. Lime, though British, has no national ties. By choice he is a man without a country. He rejects all tradition. A physician by training, he destroys human life on a large scale. His scheme of selling diluted penicillin to hospitals causes the horrible deaths of children ill with meningitis. To him these murders lack meaning. When he and Rollo Martins look down from the Big Wheel high above the Prater, the people below appear to him as insignificant dots. Martins tries hard to invest Lime with an honorific public school identity but soon comes to realize that Harry Lime is a classic psychopathic personality; people have never mattered to him. Larry Lime the school chum never existed.

The Third Man explores a familiar motif: that of the amoral agent pursuing his own ends because his culture lacks a moral center. The Russians protect Lime, but their interest in him is strictly self-serving. Calloway, the narrator, comes closest to being a normative voice, but even his decency is tarnished by his desire to catch the elusive Lime and to score at the expense of the Russians. Though Lime dies appropriately in the sewers of Vienna, certain qualities of his nature live on in Greene's later characters: his isolation, egoism, and tendency to reject any objective morality. The difference between Lime and his successors is that they have found something to value. Lime has confronted the existential problem and found only himself to love, while his later counterparts reach beyond themselves and respond to the needs of others.

In a wider context, though, Greene cuts *The Third Man* to a pattern evident in other novels yet to be written. *The Third Man* becomes a larger allegory of the postwar situation. Vienna, divided as it is, shows no promise of reunification. The Four Powers squabble among themselves. Each of the zones has its villain, in the form of Lime plus his henchmen. The political condition allows for the corruption of the innocent and the operation of amoral forces among the native populace. The running to ground of Lime is really more a triumph of bumbling determination on Martins's part than of any shift in the political climate. Killing Lime changes nothing.

The Quiet American

The Quiet American, Greene's first novel devoted almost wholly to politics, reminds one that Greene has professional roots deep in the soil of his earliest calling, journalism. He states in the introduction to the Collected Edition of this novel that his first visit to Indochina was an incidental journey from an assignment in Malaya for *Life* magazine to visit his friend Trevor Wilson, then British consul at Hanoi. This was in the winter of 1951. As with all exotic and dangerous places

NOVELS AND POLITICS 1950–1970

Indochina held a powerful attraction for Greene, one so strong it was to draw him back for three more winters, through 1955, and culminate in one of his best political novels and some of his finest reportage, in his articles on Indochina published in *Paris-Match*, the *London Magazine*, the *New Republic*, the London *Sunday Times*, and *Le Figaro*.[3]

Perhaps what makes *The Quiet American* such an important historical novel is its prescience as much as its artistry, anticipating as it does the history of Vietnam after the Geneva Accords of 1956 and the American war from 1961 through 1972. In the novel Greene succeeds in creating two major dramas, both tragic and each reinforcing the other. The first is that of this lovely, highly civilized country as it moved rapidly toward the overthrow of its French colonial lords and the resultant dangers such a political change presented to the United States, who chose as a matter of policy to regard Vietnam as the key to a free Southeast Asia. Greene's novel is set in late 1951–early 1952, a few years before Dien Bien Phu, which took place in 1954, at the beginning of the appearance of signs that the French would not be able to withstand the onslaught of the Vietminh. Within this political frame the British appear as a sympathetic but neutral party. The Americans are far more anxious and hit upon the strategy of seeking to cultivate a "third force," a native political force with sufficient support to be a viable alternative to the Vietminh, later the Viet Cong, the communist national movement led by the extremely capable Ho Chi Minh. In the novel this strategy leads to the unleashing of General Thé, an actual figure of the time, and the creation of terrible destruction in Saigon. Thé, of course, historically anticipates the Diems of the 1960s, and others after them, who were also propped up as the third force by the United States.

Within this macrocosmic drama occurs the microcosmic drama of three people caught in a love triangle that is in many ways a mirror, allegorically, of the political drama. Greene chose to continue the technique he had used so well in *The Third Man* and *The End of the Affair*, of a narrator tied closely to Greene's own person. In *The Third Man* it was Colonel Calloway, in *The End of the Affair*, Maurice Bendrix the writer. In this novel it is the British correspondent Thomas Fowler, a man about Greene's age and of his profession with, one assumes, the burden of Greene's failed but indissoluble marriage, whiling away his middle years in an unimportant but dangerous assignment, writing about a war of interest to almost no one back in England. Fowler's lover is the native girl Phuong, whose name in Vietnamese means phoenix, a name one hopes of allegorical significance for both her and her country. What begins the story is the convergence of two events, one in each drama: the sudden increase in the momentum of the war and the appearance of a CIA agent, the boyish young American Alden Pyle.

Pyle is a genuine Puritan, cool, competent, self-assured—Harvard trained, the son of a distinguished professor. Everything about him smacks of old-family American Puritanism. Imbued with an understanding of the Far East based on the facile writings of the American pundit York Harding, and particularly his book *The Advance of Red China*, Pyle tries to apply Harding's view to Indochina and causes a disaster. His loyalty to Indochina consists of nothing more than mere American self-interest, unimaginative and banal. Greene consistently plays off this do-goodism against the world-weary skepticism of Fowler, the British correspondent, who, though less seasoned in the ways of the Orient than he thinks, is light-years ahead of Pyle.

The inner story, the struggle for control over Phuong, functions as a metonymy, or representation in miniature, for the larger struggle. Phuong is the East, the Third World; Fowler the Old, and Pyle the New. She is enchantingly beautiful, but resourceful and driven by an instinct for survival. Torn between the attractions of the two men she, with the assistance of her sister Miss Hei, pursues her own interests in a way that is consistent with her nature. Pyle seemingly can offer her marriage and security. Fowler's attempt to compete is thwarted when he learns his wife will not grant him a divorce. Yet Pyle's love, with its promise of marriage, is as foolish a thing as can be, and Fowler knows it. The thought of Phuong in Boston among the Brahmins is ludicrous to him. In fact, Pyle's love, like his politics, is dangerous. His innocence is both his undoing and the undoing of those around him. His puppyish desire to "protect" Phuong is as dangerous to her as is the American desire to rescue Vietnam from the forces of communism. Like many of her compatriots Phuong sees Pyle, and America, as a fabulous solution to all her needs: marry, leave Vietnam for a magical tour—Grand Canyon, Empire State Building, and beyond. Pyle's death is as much a salvation to her as it is to Vietnam, no matter how tentative her life with Fowler might be, since it frees her from what would have been an impossible life.

Pyle's ignorance dooms him to a commitment to dead values. His is a story not so much about Indochina as it is about the dangers of innocence. It depicts the immorality that lies within the hearts and minds of those who think they know what is best. It is a lesson for East and West alike, though in this novel it is quite clear that the East learned most of the lesson long ago. How charming and innocent Phuong appears to be, yet how worldly wise she really is. How experienced Pyle assumes himself to be, yet how utterly naïve. Pyle's loyalty is foolish and dangerous, not just because of its simplistic premises, but because it is symptomatic of a state of innocence that is itself dangerous: "Innocence always calls mutely for protection when we would be so much wiser to guard ourselves against it: innocence is like a dumb leper who has lost his bell, wandering the world, meaning no harm."[4] Pyle's death is pathetic but necessary. Still more frightening is the unleashing of powerful and

NOVELS AND POLITICS 1950–1970

misunderstood political forces by people like Pyle, who are doomed by their naïveté but who threaten everyone with their technological skills and their willingness to use any means necessary to achieve their ends.

So dangerous does Fowler consider Pyle that he arranges his death by luring him into the open where the forces of the communist underground can kill him. As much as he genuinely likes Pyle and is in his debt for saving his life in the watchtower episode, and as much as he hopes that Pyle can be persuaded to abandon his belief in York Harding's "third force" thesis, he knows that Pyle will not give up and that he must be killed before he causes more harm. And so, with Fowler's assistance, Pyle dies ignominiously, suffocated in the mud, shot, beneath the bridge to Dakow.

Though the novel takes its title from Pyle, the "quiet American," in many ways its focus is really on Fowler, who, as narrator and a particularly skilled one in the cutting and layering of his story, moves from being observer to actor. Much has already been said in the criticism about the existentialist motif of the novel.[5] Pyle enters the story with a set of values and an analysis, and immediately embraces a course of action. Fowler chooses instead to watch, until what he sees moves him to act. Readers have the advantage of a wider perspective, of course, through Fowler's retrospective narrative, so that they do not really move psychologically through the experience with him. They know of Pyle's death from the outset and can place events in that context as the narrative unfolds, which permits them to savor to the fullest Fowler's skills as an observer through his reportage of the battle of Phat Diem, the French colonel's press conference, the Tanyin episode, the bombing raid out of Haiphong. All these events lie close to the actual events they are drawn from and, rather than destroy the artfulness of the narrative, enhance it by lending it that quality of immediacy that readers of historical fiction come to expect. For all his coolness and affection for Pyle, Fowler's horror at Pyle's stupidity, proceeding from his innocence, and the brutalism that lies in wait under his sentimentality moves Fowler to take steps. He is changed from observer to agent, and confronts the truth that all politics has meaning only in terms of one's willingness to become engaged, at whatever level; that in the face of such horror one must, as a moral being, accept the need to act. Fowler acts to stop Pyle's terrorism.

In some ways Greene's argument may strike political sophisticates as a little too pat. It is perhaps too simplistic to argue that the Vietnamese just want to be left alone. Yet the ultimate point of *The Quiet American* is tragic, the outcome disastrous. True, Fowler gets the answer he wants from his wife, and Pyle has been eliminated. But the future is still waiting to happen. It is still the eternal present, not the future, which Fowler lives in, as he lived in it at the opening of the novel. The close of *The Quiet American* at least offers hope in the sense that the immediate danger of Alden Pyle has been met;

but as history has proved, Pyle is only one manifesta-
tion of a national obsession with saving people from
themselves to satisfy national interests, of tragedies to
come. Pyle is, in Shakespeare's words, an image of that
horror.

Our Man in Havana

Our Man in Havana was the product of two personal
experiences: Greene's Secret Service activities of the 40s
and his visits to Cuba in the 50s, especially to Havana,
which stimulated his imagination. It was particularly
the absurdity of the contrast between the lush, immoral
atmosphere of recreational Havana and the stern morality of the Cold War environment, particularly the su-
perseriousness of the intelligence agencies, that gave
rise to this the most brilliantly comic of Greene's novels.
Havana on the eve of the Castro revolution provides a
perfect setting for an exposé of a native dictatorship,
Batista's, propped up by American imperialism.

The irascible Malcolm Muggeridge says that "everything to do with intelligence infallibly ends in farce."[6]
In *Our Man in Havana* Muggeridge's dictum is acted out.
It may well be the case that *Our Man in Havana* will
prove to be Greene's most successful spy novel, given
its artful fusion of absurdity and pathos. Though it is
not the first spy novel to create such a fusion, LeRoy
Panek rightly credits it with offering new possibilities

for the development of the genre to writers in the 60s and 70s.[8]

James Wormold, the British representative in Cuba for Phastcleaners, a vacuum cleaner business, succeeds in having himself taken on as SIS operative, replete with his own group of agents, whom he pretends to have recruited but who are in the main fictional. Wormold then dutifully prepares their reports and collects their salaries and expense money. When he becomes hard pressed for intelligence to funnel back to his desk officer in London, he hits upon the idea of peddling to London the specifications of the Atomic Pile vacuum cleaner as plans for a nuclear device, which he succeeds in doing.

Greene's portrayal of the British intelligence system, which hovers on the edge of farce, provides comic relief to the high seriousness of writers like John Le Carré and Len Deighton; it ridicules the absurd without itself becoming absurd. Anyone who questions its authenticity need only turn to Compton Mackenzie, Muggeridge, Kim Philby, and many others for hilarious accounts of real-life experiences in the secret service world.[8] Hawthorne, the agent who recruits Wormold, is a caricature of the earnest Pyle—meeting his agents in lavatories, flushing toilets to foil tape recorders, whispering out of the corner of his mouth at every opportunity. The "Interlude in London" sections of the novel, with their rather sorry comic scenes of England's spy network in action, anticipate the more sharply limned

NOVELS AND POLITICS 1950–1970

portraits of Percival and Hargreaves in *The Human Factor*
some years later.

Though the spoof of *Our Man in Havana* is achieved
skillfully, Greene pushes the story beyond farce toward
chaos. Death, brutally portrayed, keeps one from confusing the world of Jim Wormold with that of James
Bond. Wormold's naïve efforts to earn a little extra cash
cause three deaths. Cuba becomes an intelligence battle-
ground in which the innocent suffer because of the in-
competence of the British and Americans, not to mention the cruelty and corruption of the Batista regime.
The more realistic picture of espionage that has come
down in recent years has given *Our Man in Havana* a
touch of prophecy.

Essentially *Our Man in Havana* confirms Greene's
comic view as it is represented in *The Third Man* and *The
Quiet American*, where in spite of the works' moral ambiguities the fates of Lime and Pyle are predictable and
their stories leave one with a sense of closure and self-
containment. Wormold is a Fool of God, fated to come
out of this thing bobbing upright. A closer reading may
perhaps negate Greene's rather harsh criticism of himself for not dealing more full and critically with the
abuses of the Batista regime. He pleads guilty to the
charge, explaining that his purpose was to write a spoof
of the intelligence service primarily and that the comic
tone of the novel works against any serious political
aim. However, it is precisely that absurdity, refusing to

dignify such an antihuman world with the seriousness of tragedy, that creates so effectively the disgusting, venal, and sadistic world that was Batista's Cuba.

The Comedians

Greene's experiences in Haiti occupied three separate journeys to that beleaguered republic over the course of several years, the first two in 1954 and 1956 during the presidency of Paul E. Magloire and the last in 1963, in the depths of the disaster of "Papa Doc," François Duvalier. His affection for Haiti arises from an attraction Greene has always had for global hot spots and calls to mind his being drawn to Mexico in the late 1930s and to Argentina and Paraguay in the late 1960s. Haiti has all the requisites for mystery and romance: a troubled history, an exotic but grotesquely poor populace, and a bizarre combination of Catholicism and the vestiges of the West African religion, voodoo.

The culmination of Greene's experiences in this case is the longest of his novels. For a writer who is accustomed to bringing his books in at something less than three hundred pages each, *The Comedians* is an engaging but sprawling novel, with a plot that moves more ponderously than those of any of his previous books. And yet in some ways it marks a particular achievement in Greene's ability to capitalize on a political theme to an extent that he was not able to do in the earlier novels,

NOVELS AND POLITICS 1950–1970

and predicts his best political novel, yet to come, *The Honorary Consul*. The story is set in Haiti in the months prior to the return of the American ambassador in May 1964. The ambassador had been recalled for consultation by President Kennedy in May of 1961. Within the historical context of the novel this event marks a turn for the worse in Haitian politics, for, coming just at the time of Philipot's revolt, it represents a major political victory for Papa Doc.

Technically, Greene turns again, as he did in *The Quiet American*, to a first-person narrator, one Brown, son of an illicit union of a native Monegasque and an Englishman, put to school with the Jesuits and growing up parentless until a card from his long-estranged mother calls him to her home in Haiti, where he appears shortly before her death. In many ways Brown is a new version of Greene's earlier narrators; he has the world-weariness and petulant jealousy of both Fowler of *The Quiet American* and Bendrix of *The End of the Affair*. Brown is both a survivor and, in the spirit of the title of the book, a comedian, one who tries not to put too much of a stake in life and to see the absurdity of human experience. He is, like his literary forerunners Fowler and Bendrix, full of ennui, of boredom and a lack of purpose, other than his possessive love for Martha and his hatred of the Duvalier regime and all it stands for.

True to the realism of Greene's political narratives, like Fowler before him Brown provides just the right perspective on the political situation in Haiti. An outsider and a European, he gives readers "Western eyes," through which, like him, they can be horrified at what transpires in this novel, from the death of Dr. Philipot at its opening to the death of Jones at its close. Brown is without roots, the archetype of Greene's rootless protagonist, without country or patrimony other than his beloved Hotel Trianon. On the one hand he provides readers with the right kind of vision: undoctrinaire, humanistic, and feeling. To the ideologue, of course, he must appear unsatisfying as a narrator, with his lack of ideology, his rejection of political philosophy, his total lack of purpose or program. Yet for the common reader he satisfies a need to provide the view that allows readers their own judgments and allows him the degree of authenticity necessary to provide them with a credible narrative.

Brown's particular virtue as a narrator is precisely this rootlessness that allows him to be a dispassionate observer, one whose love of Haiti springs only from his enchantment with the place, not from an accident of birth or parentage. His relative anonymity as "Brown," without a Christian name, as with the names of the other members of this comedic trinity, Smith and Jones, stresses the role Greene has chosen for him. He is, like us perhaps, a person of middling convictions, nonideological, humane and sympathetic to the real heroes of the novel, the Haitians themselves.

Brown's affair with Martha Pineda, wife of the ambassador of an unidentified South American country, serves to highlight the rootlessness of Brown, though its unfortunate effect is too often to paint him as a distressingly petulant lover. In its particular way, however, it allows Brown to play the Nick Carraway to his hero Gatsby, for it is Brown's naïve stance vis à vis Martha, Dr. Magiot, Philipot, Joseph, and of course Jones that lends him credibility. In an almost Jamesian sense Brown, with his foibles, makes the perfect narrator for this story.

Of the other members of this trinity of Brown, Smith, and Jones the presidential candidate William Abel Smith and his wife, caricatured though they may be, are two of Greene's most entertaining figures and show the subtlety he can bring to his portrayal of Americans. Faulted for his critical portrait of Alden Pyle in *The Quiet American* Greene still wields a sharp pen in the portrayal of the Smiths but allows them endearing qualities that temper their idiosyncratic habits. Smith symbolizes American innocence, but he reveals a depth of humanity that was lacking in Pyle. He cares and is willing to back up his care with action, as he proves in his confrontations with the Haitian governmental authorities and particularly with the feared Tontons Macoute. For all their crackpot liberalism the Smiths symbolize in their marriage a stability and commitment that is lacking in Brown's own affair with Martha. They may be naïve, but they have something no one else has: faith in each other. Quaint as their affection might be, it is nonetheless real. In the sphere of Haiti, Smith's optimism is hopelessly at the mercy of Duvalier's corrupt government. Beyond Haiti, in Santo Domingo, his reforms stand a little more of a chance. But regardless of the outcome, his optimism and integrity are admirable for their strength.

The title of this novel, as with all Greene's titles, is significant. Throughout the book Greene plays on the idea of the comedian, both in the dramatic sense of the masker of deeper pain and in the music hall sense of the baggy-pants comic. Survivors are seen as comedians, people who understand that in order to get on in the world, particularly in a place like Haiti, one must learn to shift into various roles and to mask feelings. Above all, one must at all costs avoid showing the true person to those who cannot be trusted and to those who have the power to hurt one emotionally. The ultimate comedian in the novel is of course Jones, who pretends to be many things and who almost succeeds in bringing off his pretenses.

In the early stages of the novel Jones is presented as a highly secretive man, a soldier of fortune skilled in guerrilla warfare from his supposed experiences in Burma at the time of the Japanese occupation. The captain of the *Medea* says he is someone to be watched. He next appears in prison, having miscalculated the political situation and used a forged letter of introduction that mentions someone now in disgrace. Next one finds he has managed to extricate himself from that situation and has insinuated himself into the good graces of the Haitian government.

Ultimately he is found out and becomes Greene's archetypal fugitive. On the run from the Tontons Macoute, he is thrown into a situation in which he becomes a political martyr *malgrè lui.* In a supremely ironic twist he becomes the limping hero of the story. One discovers late in the game that he is nothing he claims to be, has almost no military experience, and is in fact a professional entertainer, a real comedian. Everything is not what he says it is; nothing is what he says it is not. What he really is is obscure to the reader, because it is obscure to Brown, who is obsessed by his fear that Jones, during his asylum in the embassy, has been sleeping with Martha. All those around Brown find Jones an extremely personable fellow, because, as they say, "He makes me laugh." Even the young Philipot finds in this absurd poseur the stirrings of a new hero for his revolution.

Like so many of Greene's characters before him, once Jones begins to act out his charade, he is caught in a role that will define him forever, in spite of his own wishes. In an almost painful gesture of slapstick Jones, after linking up with Philipot, meets his death because of his flat feet, which hold him back as his fellow revolutionaries retreat. He decides to stay and fight to the death. At the close of novel, as we are told at the beginning, Jones is celebrated as a hero of the revolution, and a stone is erected in his memory. Heroism is not in the performance but in the rhetoric or the gesture exercised in a given situation.

The true heroes of the novel should be the enlightened Haitians themselves: Dr. Philipot, his son Philipot the revolutionary, Joseph, and the kindly Communist Dr. Magiot, who symbolizes the hope of the future for Haiti. Magiot is a particularly moving figure, representing in so much of his thinking the position that Greene seems to have taken often in his own political comments. Magiot is a Communist, but he is also more importantly a humanist, dedicated through ideology to the betterment of a people and to their liberation from oppression. Whether there is any hope for Magiot's dreams is doubtful. Haiti proves a stubborn case, a country with as troubled a political history as any and with an ingrained tradition of corruption and venality almost unmatched by any political system anywhere. The actions of the Magiots and the Philipots are truly heroic, but one suspects rather futile; and as moving as is the funeral sermon of the liberation priest at the close of the novel, who preaches on the words of St. Thomas, "Let us go too, and die with Lazarus," one finds almost no comfort in this book. The Vietnamese in *The Quiet American* have a cool dignity that one expects will prevail after the Westerners get out of their way, but the Haitians seem to have little going for them. *The Comedians* presents a political world that is depressingly without redemption, in which the mise-en-scène exists merely as a stage on which to play out an existential exercise in

NOVELS AND POLITICS 1950–1970

identity-searching among the Westerners. Jones dies a martyr; Martha goes off to Lima in the company of her husband and son; and Brown assumes his new profession, undertaking, in the company of Mr. Fernandez. Haiti remains in the hands of Duvalier and the Tontons Macoute. Tragedy on a scale such as this is so absurd that one has little choice but to laugh.

The Comedians did not bring Greene's career as a political novelist to a close by any means. However, it marks a stage in development, presenting as it does such a stark picture of the possibilities of revolt and reform. To travel the road with him from the Cold War atmosphere of *The Third Man* of 1949 to the hopelessness of *The Comedians* in 1966 is to partake of a journey from the beginnings of the creation of the present political world to the effects of those origins. It remained in the later years for Greene to see that same world with even greater clarity.

Notes

1. Parts of this chapter are printed from my forthcoming essay, "Destructive Innocents and the Getting of Wisdom: Graham Greene's Post-War Spies," to appear in Vol. 2 of *Essays in Graham Greene*. I am grateful to the editors of *Essays* for their permission to reprint passages.

2. On Greene's political writing see Maria Couto, *Graham Greene: On the Frontier* (New York: St. Martin's, 1988).

3. See Wobbe, *Graham Greene: A Bibliography* (New York: Gar-

land, 1979) 205ff., for a helpful list of Greene's newspaper and magazine contributions. Excerpts from Greene's later letters to the *Times* are reprinted in Couto 223–25.

4. *The Quiet American* (Heinemann and Bodley Head, 1973) 33.

5. For a discussion of this theme see Robert O. Evans, "Existentialism in Graham Greene's *The Quiet American,*" *Modern Fiction Studies* 3 (1957): 241–48; and A. A. De Vitis, *Graham Greene* (Boston: Twayne, 1986) 108–11.

6. Malcolm Muggeridge, "Refractions on the Character of Kim Philby," *Esquire* 9 Sept. 1968: 113.

7. Le Roy L. Panek, *The Special Branch* (Bowling Green, OH: Bowling Green Popular Press, 1981) 129. Ray Shape considers this novel to be Greene's best political novel: "The Political Novels of Graham Greene," *Durham University Journal* 75 (1982): 73–81.

8. See esp. Muggeridge's anecdote in "Refractions" about making invisible ink from bird shit. Greene includes the same anecdote in *Our Man in Havana* (London: Heinemann and Bodley Head, 1970) 43.

CHAPTER FIVE

Comedy, Politics, and Fable, 1969–1980

For one who has had a tenuous grip on his life and been tormented by severe bouts of depression and thoughts of suicide, it seems that whatever deity may rule has confounded Greene's wishes and given him a long and productive career. Perhaps few of his novels since the peak years, when he produced *Brighton Rock*, *The Power and the Glory*, and *The Heart of the Matter*, will be held in as high esteem as those masterpieces. Nonetheless, in recent years his output both in quantity and quality continues to surprise his critics. Not only do the novels keep appearing; they show Greene's remarkable ability to recapitulate in new ways his earlier efforts. In the novels from his late career chosen here for discussion Greene has succeeded in addressing subjects and using forms introduced in his earlier career: the revival of comedy and entertainment in *Travels with My Aunt*, the fusion of politics and religion in *The Honorary Consul*, the return to espionage in *The Human Factor*, and the creation of moral fable in *Doctor Fischer of Geneva, or the Bomb Party*.

Travels with My Aunt

Travels with My Aunt is a brilliant comic tour de force that was anticipated by Greene's earlier success *Our Man in Havana*. In it he returns to the criteria he established earlier for his entertainments: a story with a pace that dominates the novel and a concurrent emphasis on melodrama and on action over character, and, in the tradition of melodrama, a fortunate outcome to the story. Ordinarily one expects from the entertainments a deemphasis on character, yet in *Travels with My Aunt* Greene has created two of his most memorable characters: Henry Pulling and his mother, Aunt Augusta Bertram. Contrary also to the typical plan of the entertainment, which seeks to produce a well-contrived action that in turn produces a successful result, this novel focuses on a deeper theme, that of discovery and rediscovery, though its outcome is truly fortunate—with one exception, the fate of Wordsworth.

Henry Pulling's travels with Aunt Augusta, whom he eventually discovers is his mother, have the effect of beginning a new life for both of them at fairly late and very late stages in their present lives. Henry is in his mid-fifties, and has taken early retirement from his position at the bank. In his meeting after an absence of over fifty years with Aunt Augusta, on the occasion of his mother's funeral, unbeknownst to him he is about to throw over his suburban life of retirement, raising

COMEDY, POLITICS, AND FABLE 1969–1980

prize dahlias, for a New Life in Paraguay, as a principal in a profitable smuggling operation.

The novel is a reprise of the familiar pattern of the picaresque romance, in which a character, through a series of episodes or adventures, opens his readers' eyes to certain realities in the culture that previously have lain unnoticed. In this instance, as in so many others in the picaresque tradition, the process occurs through a series of journeys: in part 1 to Brighton, to Paris, on the Orient Express through Europe to Istanbul, with a stopover in Venice, to Boulogne to visit his father's grave; in part 2, to South America, up the north-south river system, ultimately to Aunt Augusta in her New Life in Asunción, Paraguay.

Henry Pulling's goal is to discover himself and to embrace an ideal of living that values adventure and enterprise for its own sake. Of all Greene's novels this one speaks most directly to the values Greene must aspire to in his own experiences: to search for adventure and for novelty. Its controlling metaphor is that of Uncle Jo Pulling, whom Aunt Augusta describes to Henry in their visit to Brighton. When Uncle Jo realized he no longer would be able to travel as he wished, he took a villa outside Venice with fifty-two rooms (including lav), so that each week he could live in a new environment during that last year of his life. Even at the very end, when he is confined to the fifty-first room—past his weekly limit—he rebels. He is found dead in a hallway, in the act of crawling, dragging his packed suitcase toward the lav, the last room.

Henry's further purpose is to discover who he is, who his mother is. The novel opens with the death of his putative mother, Angelica Bertram Pulling, and closes with the discovery of his true mother, her sister Augusta. Through the travels, then, both figures resonate. Aunt Augusta uses the journey to rediscover for herself the life she led and to reveal this life to her son. It consists of a shady and disreputable but vivid existence, conducted through a series of love affairs. In Brighton it was Curran, the circus impresario and founder of a church for dogs. In Paris it was Mr. Achille Dambreuse, keeper of Augusta, another mistress, and a wife, all within walking distance of each other. In Venice it was the love of her life, Mr. Visconti, a scoundrelly figure, war criminal, and dealer in lost art treasures. In the trip to Boulogne it is Henry's father, who is revealed as anything but the proper man his son thought him to be. For Aunt Augusta, then, the travels represent a reevaluation and reconnection so that she can retrieve from her lost life that part of it which she wishes to live out fully—to be reunited with Mr. Visconti and take up where she ended in Venice. This act is not without pain, for it naturally means the rejection and ultimately the death of her present lover, Wordsworth. Wordsworth is one of Greene's most successful comic creations, endearing and totally human, so devoted to Aunt Augusta that he must follow her over the course of her travels and finally die in his efforts to gain back her love.

In many ways Aunt Augusta is a surer and wiser and of course older Ida Arnold of *Brighton Rock*. Her wisdom comes not just from her love of the world, which derives from Ida, but from a love that is annealed and humanized by the give-and-take of seventy-five years of living in the world. Where the fortyish Ida exhibits a simple and doctrinaire secular morality, Aunt Augusta takes the world as she finds it, responding to it partly through her own special brand of Catholicism, partly from the experience of living.

While one aim of the story is to allow Aunt Augusta to resume the life she desires for herself, its further aim is to educate Henry. It permits Henry not only to discover who his real mother is, but, once he recognizes who she is, this new knowledge allows him to begin a life true to himself and to his origins as her son. His earlier existence can only be described as prosaic at best. He has survived in his white-collar position; he has flirted with the possibility of a comfortable marriage with the spinsterish Miss Keene, and continues a barely tangible postal connection with her in her new home in South Africa. Yet he knows that what she represents is a resumption of the dull life of Southwood. Suddenly, at his mother's death, a whole new identity is his for the taking. His mother is not his mother and his father turns out to be, contrary to his knowledge of him, something of a rake. Gradually, then, in the course of travels and returns to Southwood Henry is able to claim a new identity and a new life.

Travels with My Aunt closes with the death of Wordsworth, symbolizing the death of the old life, and with Henry's recapitulation of that life: the pleasant house in Southwood, Major Charge and his goldfish, memories of his dahlias and of the unfortunate Miss Keene and her sad letters from Koffeefontein. All this closes with Henry's words, " 'I have been happy,' I said, 'but I have been so bored for so long.' " Out of a death dream he moves to the party and into his new life; he is reunited with his new-found mother, his new bride, new occupation, in a new land far from Southwood. Greene brings this wonderfully entertaining and skillfully developed story to a redemptive close, as life begins at this point for both mother and son.

The Honorary Consul

In returning to Latin America, a part of the world he had known so well artistically in his early career, Greene created in *The Honorary Consul* a powerful novel set amid the trappings of modern Third World politics: tyranny, corruption, overwhelming poverty, and terrorism. Greene has referred to it as his favorite book, one that he feels most satisfied to have written.[1] In the last measure, terrorism, it anticipates what has come to be known of both Latin American and Middle Eastern politics in the 1980s. In its locale, the small city of Corrientes and its environs, on the border between Argentina and Paraguay, it projects a political world that offers little hope of change. In point of fact it may be one of Greene's most pessimistic novels. Its strength, however, lies in the story it has to tell, about a group of people caught in a tragicomic political incident.

In Greene's work the purpose of the novelist is to reveal "real" events and characters, which are masked over by apparent events and the warped perceptions of characters by other characters in the novels. Once readers are made privy to the real natures of the characters they meet in a given story, they come to understand that there is an underlying humanity in the best of people, and that this is evidence of a basically benevolent God, that the perception of evil is exactly that, a perception, not a reality. They are given entrée to an inner truthful life that is inaccessible to the people in the novels. Greene has commented that if all were known in the life of any given individual, even the most heinous of criminals, there would be no blame, only understanding.[2] As a rule characters themselves are doomed to misunderstand because they misperceive how things occur. On the simplest level the difference between reality and illusion is a matter of dramatic irony, but seen more generally in Greene's works that irony is a profound revelation of how the world really is. Of all Greene's later novels, both in its characters and in the unraveling and outcome of the plot, *The Honorary Consul* is the strongest exponent of that irony.

As has been the custom in his other political novels Greene chose for this story a narrative perspective that offers a mix of the Old World and the New. Dr. Eduardo Plarr, half-British and half-Paraguayan (of Spanish, not native Indian, origin, however), serves as a guide through the complexities of feeling that Greene evokes here. Plarr functions as a man caught between two worlds. His father was a native Britisher, converted to and then fervently devoted to liberation politics in Paraguay. Separated from him at the age of fourteen, Dr. Plarr venerates his memory and nurtures the hope that he is still alive. His mother, a native Paraguayan with Spanish roots, was once a dark-eyed beauty, but over the years she has become an obese, fatuous woman. She lives in Argentina, in Buenos Aires, feeding her self-centeredness with the resentment she feels at having been abandoned twenty years ago by her husband for the sake of his politics. She cannot understand the missionary zeal her nonnative spouse had for the cause of liberation, and Greene captures in her character the apathy of a Latin American urban middle class that has failed to recognize its political insensitivity.

Plarr's profession, medicine, places him in a position to be exposed to all levels of South American society, but particularly it draws him to the plight of the millions of poor. At one point in the novel he puts the situation in poignant terms by describing the ability of the middle class to articulate their illnesses and discomfort, to give names to their physical suffering and hence capture some measure of control over it, while the poor suffer on inarticulately and hence are understood not at all. Plarr's experiences of life and death touch everyone from the illiterate whores at Senora Sanchez's to the elegant but culturally myopic writer Dr. Saavedra.[3] He also spans political spectra, foreign and domestic, has entrée to the British community, contact with the repressive Argentine government; most importantly he is tied closely to the Paraguayan terrorists.

In several ways Plarr reminds one of Brown of *The Comedians*. Like Brown he is a man without a country. He is also an only child, and fatherless. He is of mixed cultural background. Like Brown he is enmeshed in an adulterous affair that places him at the center of emotional conflict. Brown's affair with the mature Martha Pineda, wife to an ambassador, is, however, of quite a different order from Dr. Plarr's affair with the ex-prostitute Clara, semiliterate native of Tucumán and now the wife of the honorary consul, Charley Fortnum, for Clara is carrying Plarr's child. The expected child lends a new dimension to Greene's usually depressing, sterile adulteries. This one looks to the future and to the hope that finally is born in his later novel *The Human Factor*, in which Maurice Castle and Sarah express their love through their devotion to Sam, the child Sarah bore from a previous affair. In Plarr's response to the child there is considerable ambiguity, as there is in his feel-

UNDERSTANDING GRAHAM GREENE

ings for Clara. Yet on balance he sees the child as a positive force, as a hope. In its mixed heritage of English, Spanish, and Indian blood the child, it is hoped, will temper the old hatreds and offer a new cultural identity. It is a new kind of hostage to a world that holds who knows what kind of destiny. Yet there is a life and hence a future to be imagined.

The putative object of pursuit rather than the real one, of this novel is Charley Fortnum, a native Argentinian and second-generation English, the product of Anglo civilization. He epitomizes the failed life in all he does. He is a landowner and farmer who on his estate raises the native beverage crop, maté, while managing to maintain some semblance of a genteel but impoverished existence as a *colon manqué.* His other profession, that of honorary consul, is something of a bad joke in the end, as it enmeshes him in the Paraguayan rebels' kidnap plot quite by accident. His life consists of performing a minimum of farm-managing and ceremonial acts as honorary consul, drinking the "right measure," and looking after his cherished Land Rover, Fortnum's Pride. His first marriage, to an American from Idaho, was childless, and his estranged wife conveniently dies of cancer and hence frees him to marry Clara in the waning years of his life. His faith, Catholic, has never meant much to him. He believes Clara to be carrying his child, and he clings to life in the hope of having at last done something meaningful in fathering a child. When he is kidnapped he struggles ferociously to hold on to that life, only to find that he has been made the fool and that he has been playing the cuckold. In a bitter but comic twist, at the end of the novel it is he who survives to become a hero of sorts and be recommended for an O.B.E., which he hears Plarr refer to, in a dream, as the Order of the Bad Egg, and to become the father to Plarr's child by Clara.

One sees in him qualities of Jones in *The Comedians* and of Wormold in *Our Man in Havana*. In Greene's special teleology Fortnum proves the truth that in an absurd world things always come to an absurd close. Greene's heroes, if they can be called such, die prosaic and rather stupid deaths, while his bumblers manage to come through unscathed. Wormold ends a wealthy man, honored by his queen, while the innocent die around him. Jones, the ultimate fraud, can't escape the Tontons Macoute because his flat feet make it impossible for him to run. The whisky priest, who has no interest in martyrdom whatever, is manipulated into a martyrdom he cannot refuse. Pinkie's plans for a violent apocalypse go completely awry. Scobie makes elaborate preparations to mask his suicide, but they unravel quite easily in the face of Louise's and Wilson's astuteness. Querry dies as prosaically as any, at the hands of the despicable Rycker, for a wrong he never committed. The list is long.

The most puzzling and hence, along with Plarr, the most attractive figure in this novel is the excommunicated priest León Rivas. Typical of Greene's best characters he is a failure at almost everything he does, but especially as a priest and a revolutionary. He can most profitably be thought of as a reprise of the whisky priest from *The Power and the Glory*. At the center of all Greene's political novels the Church is always present, more so in *The Honorary Consul* than in any other. As do all Greene's books after the watershed of *A Burnt-out Case*, this one portrays a Church lost to her believers, rejected by the intelligent faithful, of value only for having in some way or another been responsible for evoking in Greene's characters a profound humanism, a belief in the worth of human beings that stands resolutely as the foe of every person or belief that seeks to pervert morals and faith in order to kill, maim, or otherwise exploit the underclass. The great devil in these political dramas that come after *A Burnt-out Case* is an exploitative capitalism that wields its power through cunning or crazed dictators like Stroessner in Paraguay, Batista in Cuba, and Duvalier in Haiti.

Rivas is a New Priest of a New Church, a Church Militant, a Church Liberated. This Church embraces the Catholicism of the masses, preaching a new social gospel of liberation from the tyranny of the Old Church and her alliances with capitalism and despotism. No longer can Latin America accept the patient Christianity of the whisky priest. This new world demands action, certainly violence, to defeat the cruel heirs of the benevolent materialism of the lieutenant in *The Power and the Glory*. Rivas is such a priest. He is out of power but still very much a priest in the eyes of his new communicants. He has taken a wife. He has adopted a philosophy of revolution and to a great extent the politics of communism, in the spirit of the hero of liberation, the martyred Cuban leader Ché Guevara. How committed and how successful he is are matters that readers must judge for themselves.

In the spirit of Greene's inept heroes and of Greene's virulent attack throughout this novel on the Latino concept of *machismo*, Rivas, on orders of his leader in Paraguay, one El Tigre, engineers a kidnapping that goes frightfully awry. The wrong man is taken, and then the whole business from that point on is so badly managed that all the terrorists are killed, including Rivas and Plarr. Yet in the spirit of the desperation the Church has put him in, Rivas makes a valiant effort to be true to his real commitment to the revolution, to Christian humanism, and to his people.

In the spirit, also, of the whisky priest's creation as an amalgam of the drunken priest Greene heard about on his visit to Mexico in 1938 and of the legendary Padre Pro, Rivas is a model of the new generation of liberation priests, reared in upper-middle-class comfort, torn between a repugnance for an uncaring Church serving the interests of the propertied class and a reverence for the true Church. Rivas's father was a prominent lawyer in Asunción; he grew up surrounded by wealth. In a prescient moment Fortnum describes him as the thumbless figure in the fairy tale of Struwwelpeter, unable to minister to the people's needs. Rivas himself sees the hypocrisy in a priest's giving out tasteless communion wafers to his flock and reserving the wine to himself. He sees the futility of trying to separate out degrees of sin, or to separate the good from the evil, and finally gives candy treats to all the children at confession regardless of their merit. In this respect he practices the total Christianity he inherited from the whisky priest.

His marriage is a pure marriage in the sense that it is a holy bond in the tradition of the sacrament, being consecrated by bride and groom alone. It is childless, where the whisky priest's lapse was not. On the other hand, Rivas sees the marriage as crucial to his ministry to all, to live as all may live and to have this sacrament opened to him, not denied him because he has chosen the priesthood. Yet his wife, Marta, like her forebear Maria of *The Power and the Glory*, is unable to think of him as anyone but a priest, and sees him not in terms of a purer faith but in the traditional terms of her religion and of *machismo*.

Like the whisky priest also, and true to his upper-middle-class roots, León Rivas is a priest who has thought deeply on the matter of the nature of God and developed a theology that, in the spirit of the French theologian Pierre Theilhard de Chardin and more recent theologians like Gregory Baum, allows for an evolving God whom believers can reconcile with the complexities of the world and with the confusion of good and evil that exists in it. Through the spirit of Rivas and his discussions with Fortnum in part 5, chapter 3, Greene provides as elaborate a discussion of the problem of evil as can be found anywhere in his fiction. Rivas views God as evolving in nature as his creation evolves, and in that sense provides an answer that up to this point Greene has been suggesting in his writing. The intuitive piety of the whisky priest has now advanced to the halting, yet unformed but still positive stance Rivas provides in these discussions.

The novel comes to completion with the rescue of Fortnum and the deaths of Rivas and Plarr. After having rejected the request of the blind peasant José to provide last rites for his dead wife, a refusal that certainly would trouble the whisky priest, who went to succor the mestizo, Rivas finally agrees to say a mass, rushes through it, and utters the ironic closing words, *Ite, missa est* (The mass has ended, go in peace), just before he meets his death. After Plarr is wounded in the leg, Rivas crawls out to him, in one last priestly act, to minister to him and to meet his own death. The act is at once a profound acceptance and an affirmation.

The epilogue only affirms the irony and absurdity of this drama. At Dr. Plarr's funeral, despite Fortnum's valiant efforts to set the record straight, Dr. Saavedra recites his eulogy lauding the *machismo* of Plarr, his bravery and heroic death at the hands of the terrorist Rivas. Politically, of course, nothing has changed—exactly the message of the earlier novels; but there is in Fortnum, in Plarr's child, and in the reader's having been made a participant in the complexities of the political and religious experience of this novel some hope for an evolving sense of love in the world.

The Human Factor

The Human Factor synthesizes much that had already been foreshadowed in three of Greene's earlier works in the espionage genre: the solipsism of *the Third Man*, the innocence of *The Quiet American*, and the absurdity of *Our Man in Havana*. But the atmosphere has changed and the outcome is far more ambivalent and disturbing. Both the absurd and the tragic elements of espionage are drawn together in what must be considered Greene's most ambitious spy novel to date.

The Human Factor tells of three people isolated in an alien technocracy. Maurice Castle, a "turned" agent now working for the Russians, finds himself on the verge of being exposed and must escape to Russia and leave behind his black South African wife, Sarah, and her young son, Sam. It is apparent that Castle and Kim Philby share identities in that both are proven to be turned agents, who live double lives until they are threatened with exposure and then defect to Russia. Clearly, Philby served Greene as the model for Castle. Yet despite the similarities between Castle and Kim Philby the men differ in their essential natures.

In his preface to Philby's *My Silent War*, Greene's

sympathetic portrayal of Philby hinges on his belief that his man was working for a higher cause.[4] Castle, however, is moved mostly by his personal commitment to Sarah, Sam, and Carson, the communist agent who helped Sarah escape from South Africa. He feels committed to the liberation of Sarah's people, but he is not a communist. Only grudgingly does he admire the old party worker who has served through the years as his cutout, or "contact." Margaret Scanlan's judgment that Greene's portrayal of Kim Philby in Castle is the most successful to date is well taken; her perceptive analysis of the points of contact between the two figures, one real and the other fictional, more than accounts for the similarities they share, and also for their divergences.[5] Instead of immersing himself in causes, Castle has spent his later years looking for emotional ties, has found them, and made a deep commitment to Sarah and her child. The novel's epigraph, taken from Conrad's *Victory*, states that "he who forms a tie is lost. The germ of corruption has entered his soul." Castle's life since meeting Sarah has been shaped, or rather doomed, by his tie to her. What it is to be lost and what it is to be corrupted are deliberate ambiguities, however. Harry Lime escaped this fate, while Castle has become trapped by it, sitting in his apartment in Moscow and gazing at the red star that shines over the nearby university and illuminates the oppressive and endless spread of Russian snow below.

The "human factor" of the novel's title, on one level,

is the dooming connection of the love tie. For the Firm it is simply an element, a "factor" to be manipulated. On another level, in an equivocation that American readers might miss, the Firm is indeed a "factor," a broker in the commodity of human life. *The Human Factor* exposes the Secret Service's casual bureaucrats who plan great enterprises affecting human life during grouse-shooting weekends in the country or over lunches at private clubs in the West End. These "operatives" work in a milieu that seems unreal, where their decisions have surprising and usually horrible effects.

The catastrophe of this novel is heavily ironic. Castle defects to Russia, intending to have Sarah and Sam follow, but the British foil his plan. After he arrives in Moscow, he discovers that his work in London served no real purpose. He had been used by MI5 to feed false information to a double agent in Moscow, who had not actually turned but who was still working for the Russians. This agent then sent the information back to London, along with false information the Russians wanted the British to accept as authentic. Castle discovers he was not a great double agent but only a minor figure in an espionage shadow play. He has escaped to a country he has no love for, Russia, where he must abandon the two people he loves, Sarah and Sam.

His predicament constitutes Greene's severest condemnation of the System. Castle is caught in a trap of them-us, and his cleverest efforts to escape from it are thwarted. There is an exit, but it leads to isolation. *The*

COMEDY, POLITICS, AND FABLE 1969–1980

Human Factor says that the state, as it expresses its morality in espionage, has no regard for human values. It is locked in a struggle largely of its own creation, one that has little relevance to the lives of ordinary citizens. To Castle "country" means the Firm, and when he must decide whether he should be loyal to the Firm and condone their support of a repressive South Africa regime or whether he should reveal their plans and thus help millions of black South Africans, he does not hesitate to betray the Firm. His ultimate loyalty is to people—to the blacks, to Sarah, to Sam. Loyalty in the end must mean a commitment to humanity, not to empty words, impersonal bureaucracies, or facile emotions.

The Human Factor is Greene's culminating fictional design in the spy genre, as it synthesizes all the foregoing espionage motifs in one narrative statement. Castle and his world embody the elements analyzed in a lesser way in the previous novels, allowing Greene the opportunity not only to reflect on issues he raised in the earlier works but also to reshape them into a more comprehensive whole. The SIS operation in *The Human Factor* is just as harebrained as the one in *Our Man in Havana*. The self-righteous destructiveness of Hargreaves and Percival echoes that of Pyle. Castle is as alone in the end as Harry Lime was, but his predicament is quite the reverse of Lime's, who found himself alone because he could not reach beyond himself. Castle reaches beyond, and his efforts cut him off from those he loves. He is caught in a struggle between two powerful bureaucracies from which no escape is possible. To avoid being the victim of one intelligence network he puts himself at the mercy of another and becomes its prisoner. Greene's final vision is a horrifying one of a world riddled with fear and isolation—the end of all innocence.

Doctor Fischer of Geneva

Doctor Fischer of Geneva, or the Bomb Party marks a return for Greene to the surrealistic fable. As he intimates in his dedication of this remarkable novella, the story grew out of one told over a Christmas dinner. Its starkness and its exploration of the bizarre seem appropriate to its pleasantly familial origins, which belie a tale of greed and sadism. Greene introduces his rather unprepossessing narrator as Alfred Jones, a middle-management type in a Swiss chocolate firm, over sixty years old at the time of narration but in his late fifties at the time of the events of the story. One may well look for correspondences between this Jones and Jones of *The Comedians*, and though they appear to be unrelated in most ways, they do share a common identity as Greene's rather faceless, identityless narrators of the later novels of his career.

The story is set appropriately enough in Geneva, a city traditionally associated with peace and compromise. The texture of the story and the qualities of its central character are reminiscent of the earlier *England Made*

Me. The prototype of Fischer is Erik Krogh. Both have made their fortunes from products that meet a particular need, Krogh from his industrial cutter, Fischer from his dentifrice. As was Krogh, Fischer is a sociopath, from whose gross selfishness this bizarre story derives; it is not, as was *England Made Me*, a complex anatomy of the psychology of the reclusive tycoon, but rather a moral fable on the effects of greed.

Fischer is a modern reincarnation of Robert Browning's Duke of Ferrara, of his poem "My Last Duchess." In it the duke, in the course of arranging a new marriage for himself, speaks to an emissary from the prospective bride's family. The poem is a revelation of the extent to which pride can warp a man. Fischer's possessiveness of Anna, his wife and mother to Anna-Luise, the new wife of the narrator Jones, rivals that of the duke, who in order to control totally the whole person of the duchess (who, as the first line implies, is only one among several) finally orders her death in some unspecified manner. It is not that Anna was unfaithful to Fischer, but rather that she preferred the lowly company of the clerk Steiner. Moreover, she preferred the company of someone who was not rich, the deepest offense. To throw into contrast Fischer's perverted sense of loss Greene provides a parallel to Fischer's loss of Anna in Jones's loss of Anna-Luise in a skiing accident. Where Fischer is seemingly not touched by his wife's death, Jones is totally distraught by the death of his wife and turns to thoughts of suicide.

Fischer's response is quite the opposite. Instead, he creates a depraved little *ludus,* or game, of greed for five sycophants whom he has managed to gather about him. The five endure petty humiliations at Fischer's dinner parties in order to receive from him lavish gifts, which they then either redeem or keep. Greed feeds greed, and both Fischer and his "Toads," as Anna-Luise calls them, reinforce each other's worst qualities.

With the death of Anna-Luise the stage is set for the climactic event of the novel, Fischer's grand party, at which the ultimate test of the Toads' greed will be carried out. Simultaneously the party brings to a climax the conflict between Doctor Fischer and Jones. The party's surrealistic qualities—the subzero outdoor setting, the four enormous bonfires, and the lights hanging from the trees—all create the effect of a bizarre dreamlike atmosphere and heighten the ghoulish characteristics of the Toads. The setting is reminiscent of Dante's lowest circle of hell in the *Inferno,* the frozen lake of Cocytus. The conditions of this game allow the participants to engage in a high-risk gamble, their lives against a check for two million Swiss francs, with the odds six to one in favor of their drawing a check. Each participant is to reach into a barrel filled with sawdust, in which are buried six "crackers," or small paper toys, party favors that contain usually a paper hat. When the ends of the cracker are pulled, it opens with a loud noise to reveal the toy. Five of Fischer's crackers contain the checks; one is supposedly a bomb. For Jones the odds are quite against him, since he prefers death to anything. But of course such is not to be, and as he realizes he is not to die, he feels Anna-Luise walking away from him. The real danger for Jones is in the money, as Doctor Fischer states, which is the beginning of his corruption.

When Jones takes an extra cracker and the game begins to disintegrate, there is only one cracker left, which Jones then "purchases"; but it too is harmless, so that in his greed for death he is as much duped by Doctor Fischer as are the others. The outcome for Doctor Fischer is perfect; he has made fools of each one of them, Jones as well.

With the end of the party, however, and the appearance of Steiner to remind Fischer of his own vacuous existence, despair washes over him, and he goes off by himself and commits suicide, the only meaningful act now that his plans for his Toads and for Jones have come to fruition. Ironically, it is he who is most in despair. Jones lives to die; the others live to possess; but Fischer lives for no reason at all now. He has found the death Jones did not have the courage to seek. The novel closes with an epilogue in which Jones informs the reader of the fates of the Toads, who appear to have continued their empty lives, and of his own, which has achieved a stasis not satisfying but welcome, given the fact that death is not a choice he can make.

Notes

1. Marie-Françoise Allain, *The Other Man: Conversations with Graham Greene* New York: Simon and Schuster, 1983) 129. He ranks it above *The Power and the Glory* because he is more satisfied with the dynamism he has instilled in the characters, whereas he believes the figures in *The Power and the Glory* tend to be static. The judgment must be thought of strictly as evidence of a novelist's satisfaction with the practice of his art, not necessarily a judgment shared by a wide and discerning readership.

2. Allain 151.

3. Miriam Allott provides an excellent analysis of Saavedra's role in the novel: "Surviving the Course, or a Novelist for All Seasons: Graham Greene's *The Honorary Consul,*" *The Uses of Fiction: Essays in Honour of Arnold Kettle,* ed. Douglas Jefferson and Graham Martin (Milton Keynes, England: Open University Press, 1982) 237–48.

4. In his recent account of the Philby conspiracy Anthony Boyle disputes this view; see *The Fourth Man* (New York: Dial, 1979). The English edition is titled *The Climate of Treason,* to avoid at that time a possible libel action from Anthony Blunt. See also H. R. Trevor-Roper, *The Philby Affair* London: William Kimber, 1968), which is also unsympathetic to Greene's view.

5. Margaret Scanlan, "Philby and His Fictions," *Dalhousie Review* 62 (1983): 537–45.

CHAPTER SIX

Short Stories, Plays, Essays

Stories

Graham Greene is one of the most successful short story writers of all time. Very few writers achieve the ability to rivet readers' attention to a dramatic situation, turn it into meaning through ingenious manipulations of plot, and in the end leave them astonished, breathless. His range is extensive, moving from the introspective to the bizarre to the shocking. Greene's output is contained in five collections, issued from 1935 through 1967: *The Basement Room and Other Stories* (1935), *Nineteen Stories* (1947), *Twenty-One Stories* (1954), *A Sense of Reality* (1963), and *May We Borrow Your Husband? and Other Comedies of the Sexual Life* (1967). These were subsequently brought together into one volume, *Collected Stories* (1972). In addition, several uncollected stories have appeared. Eighteen of the stories were filmed for the series *Shades of Greene*, produced by Thames Television in 1976 and shown over the Public Broadcasting System in the United States, with the simultaneous publication of a collection by that title. Three of the stories may suffice to reveal the prevailing techniques and themes of Greene's short fiction: "The Basement Room," "The Destructors," and "Under the Garden." All three were made into films for the *Shades of Greene* series.

"The Basement Room" first appeared as the lead and title story in Greene's first published collection, in 1935. In 1948 it was released as a film, and a highly successful one, under the title *The Fallen Idol*, directed by Carol Reed, who also directed *The Third Man*. "The Basement Room" serves as a guide to the major themes of many of Greene's novels: the innocence of childhood and its subsequent corruption when it confronts the adult world; the insidious nature of evil and its mixture with good; the relative impotence of good in the face of evil; and, most significantly, the inevitability that trust will be rewarded with betrayal, no matter how unintended that betrayal might be.

Greene chooses to narrate this story from a third-person-limited point of view, from the vantage point of the main character Philip's deathbed, sixty years after the events of the story, and to focus subtly one's attention on the lifelong impact of this episode on Philip, who has never forgotten it and who must live with its effects until his dying day. In "The Basement Room" the situation concerns then seven-year-old Philip and two household servants, Baines and Mrs. Baines, to whom he has been given over during "a fortnight's holiday." Philip is isolated from his parents and "between nurses," which means that he must, from the context of childhood, deal prematurely with an adult world of marital hatred, duplicity, and adultery, and must make crucial choices as to how to maintain allegiances that the adults require of him.

With its five sections the story is reminiscent of Renaissance tragedy, carrying its construct of rising action, crisis, falling action, and catastrophe, out of which a new awareness, however dim, arises for both protagonist and reader. The story focuses on one crucial event, the accidental death of Mrs. Baines, and its test of Philip's loyalty and his ability to interpret the event within the context of adult morality. The crisis occurs with the surprise return of Mrs. Baines to the house, where she catches Baines and Emmy *in flagrante.* It only remains for the catastrophe of Philip's betrayal to occur, and its result: the misinterpreting of Mrs. Baines's death by the police and the downfall of Baines and Emmy.

The focus of the story is on Philip; its narrative technique binds the readers to him, although they do not discover fully the narrative situation until the close of the story. What happened there on that day succeeded in some unconscious way of killing all Philip's innocence and destroying his childhood love of life. His innocence has no difficulty dealing with Mrs. Baines's clearly malicious nature; it fears it, while it betrays Baines both at the end of the story and earlier, when Mrs. Baines discovers the crumb of pink sugar on his lapel. Emmy, the young girl who is Baines's lover, is a great mystery to Philip throughout his life, and he dies with the question on his lips he has asked himself over and over again for the past sixty years: Who is she? The answer is that she is, like her descendant Rose in *Brighton Rock*, the potentiality for love and happiness, but she is so frail and identityless that she cannot survive in a world in which the force of evil is so strong that it traps the good (Baines) and subverts the innocent to its own cause (Philip). Philip dies an old, loveless man, never having created anything, and carrying with him the unforgettable memory of Mrs. Baines's shrill voice, a voice he could mimic with devastating effect.

The story closes with the death of innocence, the powerful sickness of the heart induced by Philip's betrayal, and foreshadows future stories to be written: *Brighton Rock* and Rose's goodness, that also of Sarah Miles in *The End of the Affair* and of Bendrix's opacity; of Scobie's innocence in *The Heart of the Matter*, and that of Pyle in *The Quiet American*, the deadliest innocent. Philip, too, as a child foreshadows all Greene's children, from the childlike Pinkie and Rose, to Coral Fellows and the Mexican boys, to the shrieking child in *The Third Man*, who almost does in Rollo Martins.

"The Destructors" first appeared serialized in two parts in *Picture Post*, July 24 and 31, 1954. Its first appearance in a collection was in *Twenty-One Stories* in 1954. Perhaps no story since Shirley Jackson's "The Lottery" appeared in *The New Yorker* in 1948 has produced such a disturbing effect on readers. Next to "The Base-

SHORT STORIES, PLAYS, ESSAYS

ment Room" it has attracted more critical attention than any other story by Greene, and is his most frequently anthologized story. "The Destructors" may be Greene's best story and perhaps one of the finest in the language. It has all the qualities that have come to be expected in the short story: focus, compression, pace, and that element of surprise, that epiphany that brings one to recognizing a powerful truth. It works as both parable and allegory, parable in the sense that it is a narrative in a relatively contemporaneous setting that makes a clear moral point, allegorical in the sense that it "signifies" on several levels.

As parable the story is a mirror of experience which reflects the condition of England during the immediate postwar period, at a time when England was only gradually recovering from the destruction of the blitz and the ravages more generally of the war. The locale, Wormsley Common, has been bombed, and the house of Mr. Thomas (a.k.a. "Old Misery") sticks up like one last sound tooth in a rotten mouth. More significantly, the house symbolizes the traditions of civilization, having been designed and built by the distinguished seventeenth-century English architect Christopher Wren; yet these traditions have not been upheld over the years, and readers know that Old Misery has been sadly remiss, as have others before him, in their obligation to maintain the edifice in its proper style. The young protagonist, Trevor, or T., as he prefers to be called, sees the rude absurdity of the grand house, and he persuades his gang of boys to set themselves the task of reducing it to rubble, not by destroying it but rather by systematically gutting it and weakening its structure, so that at the close of the story it only requires the tug of the lorry at one corner of the foundation to bring the whole structure down. Old Misery, locked in his outdoor toilet, emerges to find complete destruction. It is a horrendously cruel trick to pull on an old man, but the lorry driver says at the end, "There's nothing personal, but you got to admit it's funny." The younger English generation has succeeded in extending the actions of the older to their logical conclusion, and the landscape of Wormsley Common has rational consistency now that the Wren house is gone.

At one level readers, especially older readers, with their powerful sense of the sanctity of property, react in horror to what the gang achieve. But a deeper reading of the story reveals that much more is at stake here than property; it is the loss of a work of art, the destruction not just of a building but of a wonderful idea poorly stewarded, the loss more generally of an entire culture, not to war alone but to the wanton destructiveness of a new generation who are products of that war and have no understanding of and little stake in preserving that which they do not love.

What is perhaps more appalling than the destruction is the manner in which it is carried out. T. is caught up in both a struggle for and an exercise of power and in a rejection of his heritage, of his father, a former

SHORT STORIES, PLAYS, ESSAYS

architect, and of his mother, with her class snobbery. Politically the story is a microcosm of the acquisition and uses of power as T. succeeds in wresting control of the gang from Blackie and shapes it and motivates it to carry out his plan. What is most unsettling is that such skill and intellect are exercised by the gang in carrying out their plan. The dinnertime harangues from parents about the value of work and of dedication bear ironic fruit in their efforts.

Most powerful in the story's impact is its multilayered allegory that allows readers to see this not only as a parable on the bitter fruit of the postwar generational struggle; in a broader context it represents the death of property in a class struggle between the custodians of that property and a newer generation that sees the absurdity of that concept. On a political level it is an allegory on totalitarianism and the fruits of power, and the way in which that power, once unleashed, is difficult to control and assumes a life of its own. In another sphere it is the corruption and destruction of the good by a Manichean evil that is present in the world, ready to use those who have some small impulse toward harm and to assume a power even greater than that of those who pursue evil ends. In "The Second Coming" Yeats says, "The best lack all conviction, while the worst / Are full of passionate intensity." Greene's story is saying much the same thing here. "The Destructors" will remain a disturbingly powerful story and take on even more significance as time passes.

UNDERSTANDING GRAHAM GREENE

"Under the Garden" is Greene's longest story and, given its length, ought perhaps to be thought of as a novella. It first appeared in 1963 in *A Sense of Reality*. This story is as seminal a piece of Greene's fiction as any he has written. It brings together motifs of childhood and adulthood, of the meaning of literature and art, of the interplay of the conscious and unconscious life and the significance of dreams as clues to a character's nature, of the nature of myth and its meaning in real life—all major concerns in Greene's work. Additionally, it combines the strategies of three of Greene's favorite works, two of them, appropriately, children's books: the geography of *Alice in Wonderland*, the escape motif of Henry James's "The Great Good Place," one of Greene's favorite stories, and the romance of Robert Louis Stevenson's *Treasure Island*. It is at the same time one of Greene's most puzzling stories and one of his richest.

Structurally the story is multilayered. It relies on three separate narrations: that of the writer Greene, following his character William Wilditch through the trauma of learning that he has life-threatening, probably terminal lung cancer and his escape to his brother's estate, Winton Hall; that of Wilditch as a thirteen-year-old, recapturing and romanticizing a childhood dream through his story "The Treasure in the Island," printed in his school magazine *The Warburian* under the nom de plume "W. W." (for which one may surely substitute "G. G."); and that of Wilditch as an adult as he rewrites

SHORT STORIES, PLAYS, ESSAYS

the childhood story into a new version, the product of accretions over the fifty years since the time he had the original dream about his subterranean experience.[1] Three separate voices, three separate stories, all drawn from one source: a dream of a most compelling kind, one that has drawn its dreamer back to it time after time, since the age of seven to the present, when he is now past fifty-seven.

The geography, taken as it is from Lewis Carroll's story, provides a parallel to the dream, for it is a journey into a new land, a timeless underground world that exists below the estate garden, accessible only by squeezing into an entrance beneath a tree root on an island in the middle of a lake. It is also an escape in the Jamesian tradition because it represents a release from the pressures of the world above, where life sucks out vitality and where, in the final version of the story, Wilditch, like his author Greene, looks back over a life of travel to escape and confront certain realities, only to wonder if he has lived at all.

In the original story—that is, the childhood story of part 1, section 5—W. W. moves quickly through the experience to the discovery of treasure, but in his later version the treasure Wilditch discovers is of little avail. The "golden po" turns out to be an old chamber pot, painted yellow. In the second story the adventure of the cave far overshadows the treasure. The cave is inhabited by primeval parents, Javitt and Maria, both eternal but both maimed physically and symbolically, Javitt by being partially immobilized because he 'lacks one leg, Maria lacking the power of speech because of her lack of a palate. The one sits and speaks wisdom from his toilet seat, as Wilditch says, like a great prophet; the other races about screaming nonsense. And all this is the product of a childhood dream, written up some years later by the dreamer, mulled over during a lifetime and then rediscovered and written up again. What began as a relatively straightforward but imaginative adventure story has turned into a Freudian fable of significant proportions. Wilditch, facing what seems to be his imminent death, after a lifetime of travel in all parts of the world returns to this single experience to find meaning in it. What he discovers is that he has taken the "facts" of reality and converted them into a new reality for himself. Ernest the gardener becomes the source for much of Javitt, the garden becomes the world, and Friday's Cave and Camp Indecision become efforts on Wilditch's part, at two separate times in his life, to analyze his life and re-create that analysis as narration.

Efforts have been made to unravel this seemingly slightly disguised roman à clef, and most certainly will continue.[2] What is more important to one's understanding of it is its way of dealing with reality and the reconstitution of reality through art. What Greene does here is remarkably similar to what one sees in the allegorical layerings of his best novels. To put it in Wilditch's own words (hence Greene's): "A puddle can contain a continent, and a clump of trees stretch in sleep to the world's edge."[3] In other words, one can sense a truth as broad as the world in a story as confined as Wilditch's. More importantly, it is the life of art and the making of it that is most important, as the story proves its own point. Wilditch's mother, determined to kill all vestiges of the imaginative impulse in him, failed miserably, where the gardener Ernest succeeded by providing him with a character, and the pond and the little hillock provided a place for a powerful creative experience. And at the end of the story Wilditch, having returned to his island and found the old chamber pot, is overcome by a curiosity that can only be satisfied by rethinking and rewriting his story, yet again. A new understanding and new experiences demand a new narration. "Across the pond the bell rang for breakfast and he thought, 'Poor mother—she had reason to fear,' turning the tin chamber-pot on his lap" (237).

Plays

Greene's fascination with the theater goes back to his early writing career, when he turned out, as he says, several one-act plays, in the hope that someone might be interested in producing one of them. In 1920, at the age of sixteen, he submitted a play to one of the many dramatic societies then active in London, only to discover, after the play had been accepted, that the society was something of a sham. In one of the several interviews that Marie-Françoise Allain conducted with Greene that comprise the book, *The Other Man*, Greene says about his interest in the drama: "I think [the theater is] a necessary release from the solitude of being a novelist," and he remarks pointedly in his comments on his plays about the excellent training and discipline to be derived from writing for the stage.[4] Like many novelists before and after him and certainly in the tradition of several of the writers dear to him, Greene has cultivated a deep interest in both theater and film, and that interest he has expressed by creating eight plays over a period of thirty years, three of them having been staged or published since 1981.[5] The plays cover a broad range of dramatic presentation from serious domestic melodrama to farce and complement the breadth of his fiction, though his best theater is in the tradition of the late nineteenth-century playwrights Henrik Ibsen and Anton Chekhov, in its treatment of themes of social and religious import, using subtle and carefully textured dialogue. Greene's best plays allow for a heightened tension created by what the characters do not say or say incompletely as much as by what they are willing to say plainly. All his plays have been brought together in a complete edition, *Collected Plays*.

In addition, Greene's excellent critical book on the English theater, *British Dramatists*, published in 1942, is further evidence of his deep interest in the history of drama, particularly Elizabethan and Jacobean drama. Further, from its earliest appearance his fiction has shown

SHORT STORIES, PLAYS, ESSAYS

clearly the mark of the theater, particularly in its realistic, presentational dialogue and in the extensive use Greene makes of dramatic structure in developing his plots. Of the body of plays, the two that perhaps best reveal his dramatic skills and also throw light on his other writing are the two earliest, *The Living Room* and *The Potting Shed*.

The Living Room opened at Wyndham's Theatre in London on 16 April 1953. In a somewhat low period for the British theater, in the years after the war, it proved to be an immediate success. The play can best be described as a domestic tragedy, with the issue of adultery at its center, from which radiate themes of death, the nature of God, the nature of sin. The play is finely balanced in its set of characters, seeking to present a microcosm of human experience in the little group of people who find their lives thrown into turmoil by the affair between Michael Dennis and Rose Pemberton. Greene's penchant for the exact detail and the elusive meaning holds sway in the play, much as it does throughout his novels. Three separate "ages of man" are figured here: youth, in Rose Pemberton, age "about twenty"; middle age, in Michael Dennis, aged forty-five, and his wife, Marion; and old age in the Brownes, whose ages range from sixty-five (James) to seventy-eight (Teresa).

Out of the occasion of her mother's death Rose Pemberton clutches at life through an affair with Michael Dennis, and closes the play with her own death by suicide. She is the most vital, most promising character in the play and at the beginning exhibits many of the strengths of her namesake Rose Wilson in *Brighton Rock*. As the play progresses, however, she moves through various stages of growth, conflict, and finally desolation, to death itself. She is witty, vibrant, hopeful, somewhat immature, too; but among the dying Brownes and Michael, who is drawn more to the dying than the living, she represents the viewers' best chance for happiness. Touched by the spirit of Ophelia she has such a great care for those to whom she brings unhappiness that she chooses the escape that death provides rather than prolong her and their pain.

Her lover, Michael, is a lecturer in psychology at the University of London and former protégé of John Pemberton, Rose's dead father, a professor of psychology at the University. Of everyone in the play he stands to be most capable, through his training and expertise in the study of psychology, of dealing with the crisis. Yet he is not. He looks in one direction to the courage of youth as he sees it figured in Rose, but he is a creature of his own age. Ineluctably he is drawn in the other direction in time, in his concern for his wife and his recognition of what lies further on in life as he sees it figured in the Brownes. A nominal Protestant, in him Greene has created the representative middle-aged man who has come through tragedies of his own, much similar to those of Scobie in *The Heart of the Matter*, devoid of faith, except for what little faith he has in his field of expertise and in his own instincts, tied to a dead marriage from which he cannot extricate himself. Of anyone in the play he must accept much of the blame for Rose's death. He has his opportunity to move toward a new life, but when the old patterns lie before him, he cannot, either because of habit or guilt, break away.

The three elderly sisters and brother, Helen, Teresa, and James Brown, fail most deeply and at various levels among themselves. They symbolize a rejection of life, to varying degrees, and the substitution of fraudulent ritual and an escape into a literal-minded religious faith as ways of dealing with life. The least culpable is Teresa, the oldest, whose only fault is her passivity, while Helen and James carry a heavy burden of guilt. Their last contact with their grandniece Rose was fourteen years ago, when she was a lively six-year-old, and even then they only tolerated her presence. Now that their niece, Rose's mother, is dead, Rose comes back among them as an "orphan," a ward of James and Michael. She is now a beautiful woman, mature in mind and body, but also an adulteress. Symbolic of their collective ambience is the room from which the play takes its title and in which all its action occurs. Formerly an upstairs bedroom, it has now been converted to a living room because it is a room in which, as best they can determine, no one has ever died. To avoid death and create the illusion of life the Brownes have closed off the rooms in which people have died. This living room, ironically, is the room in which Rose kills herself. After her death Teresa, previously a harmless, senile old woman submissive to Helen's will, finally asserts herself and proclaims that she will be moving her bedroom into this living room, because "there'd be no better room for me to fall asleep in for ever than the room where Rose died."[6] This defiant act horrifies Helen, who is really the perpetrator of this scheme of closing the rooms.

The two maleficent figures in the play are Marion Dennis and Helen Browne. Marion is the conventional wife spurned, with some humanizing touches. Helen, however, is more complex. She is a figure of great power, though she assumes herself to be a typically morally upright, thoroughly conventional believing Catholic. Over the years it is she who has been in control. She has affinities with Ida Arnold of *Brighton Rock* in her "conventionalist" attitude toward her faith, toward human feelings. She lives the Right Life of the typically devout spinster Catholic woman, proud of her heritage and determined to see it prevail. It is she who is directly the cause of the unraveling of this play through her determination to sabotage Rose's affair with Michael. This she achieves at the close of Act I by claiming to need Rose to care for the ill Teresa, and in Act II by inviting Marion Dennis to the house. That event puts the remainder of the action into motion. At the end of the play she has only death to look forward to, as her control has been wrested from her with Teresa's defiant act.

Father Browne may be Greene's most interesting

SHORT STORIES, PLAYS, ESSAYS

"conventional" priest. His invalid condition is both symbolic and real. For years he has been confined to a wheelchair, having lost both his legs at the knees in an auto accident. He is waiting, as he says, for the moment when God will provide him with an opportunity to put his faith to work. During these three weeks in January in which the action occurs, that moment comes, but all he can do is urge Rose to turn to conventional Catholic devotions, to prayer for help. Rose's incredulous response, "Prayer!" toward the close of Act II, Scene i, has an effect akin to Nora's slamming of the door in Ibsen's *A Doll's House*. The impact is astounding and signals to Father Browne what a failure he is and what a failure his formulaic faith is in the face of a genuine moral dilemma. It takes Rose's death to purify his own faith and allow him to give voice to the humanitarian feelings toward that faith that he has been trying to express for many years.

The outcome of *The Living Room* is heavily ironic and tragic, but it is not without a certain redemptive quality. Rose's death has brought these unfortunate people—as always, too late—some measure of understanding of what it means to be genuinely human and loving, and how killing dead creeds, rigid tenets, false values, and rationalistic beliefs can be. Rose is lost to them, but they have a deeper knowledge of themselves, an understanding that living involves loving and dying, not simply enslaving oneself to a life-denying religious code.

The Potting Shed opened at the Bijou Theatre in New

UNDERSTANDING GRAHAM GREENE

York on 29 January 1957. It proved to be far more successful in America than its predecessor, which closed after a dismal Broadway run. Dramatically and thematically *The Potting Shed* represents an advance over Greene's successes in *The Living Room*. Where the earlier play ends tragically, with a brief sense of stasis, and where one's sense of loss is great, the focus of this play is stronger, its development more focused on the crucial process of discovery, and its outcome is more positive. The intense focus of the play on the religious theme makes it Greene's last major work of faith, soon to be followed by a change of direction, already foreshadowed by *The Quiet American* but to be given full expression in *A Burnt-out Case*. Coming in 1957, it gathers together themes that Greene had been handling in novels and stories up to that time. Here one finds a great deal of autobiography. Greene has returned to Nottingham, the world of *A Gun for Sale*, and his life as a down-at-the-heels journalist. The teen-age suicide is very much drawn from Greene's own adolescent experiences, as he details them in *A Sort of Life* and elsewhere.[7] From his imaginative writing this play recalls several characters and their crises. James Callifer's loss of his memory of his childhood is reminiscent of Arthur Rowe's loss of memory in *The Ministry of Fear*. James's father, Henry, and his uncle William constitute two poles of belief around which the events of the play circle, just as Greene had created two spokespersons in the whisky priest and the lieutenant in *The Power and the Glory*. Father Cal-

SHORT STORIES, PLAYS, ESSAYS

lifer's sacrifice is very much akin to that of Sarah Miles in *The End of the Affair*, where, after the bomb explosion in the flat, Sarah gives up her love for Bendrix so that he might live.

Structurally the play has a classical, almost Sophoclean quality, as the action revolves totally about a discovery, and the discovery controls the effect of the play. Greene succeeds in unraveling the mystery of what happened in the potting shed in a manner that is both dramatically and thematically effective. The play's time frame is March and April of 1956; its setting moves from Wild Grove, to Nottingham, to an East Anglian village, back to Wild Grove. In that limited time and those places the events of a particular day in 1925 are reconstructed, in three stages, through three "witnesses." For everyone in the play but James and his niece Anne, and the audience, what occurred on that day is no secret. The first witness is Mrs. Potter, who speaks for her dead husband, the gardener. Potter discovered James, presumably dead, hanging in the potting shed. What his wife provides are the spare facts: that James had hanged himself and that Potter believed him to be dead. With her information in hand James then confronts his uncle, Father William Callifer, in his rectory in a secluded village in East Anglia, where his uncle reveals to him the crucial details of what occurred: that, finding James dead, William prayed to God that in exchange for his faith God restore James to life. Immediately James began to breathe. In Father Callifer's dreary rectory James sees that in one way or another his uncle has paid the price, creating a hell of lost faith for himself, having to practice a hollow vocation that he can only endure by retreating into drink. The final stage of the revelation takes place back at Wild Grove, where the events are once again reviewed by Dr. Baston, who seeks to reaffirm a thoroughly rational view of James's revival, but his interpretation is put into doubt by James, who believes in the efficacy of his uncle's sacrifice. A further piece of information from Baston brings the play full circle when he reveals that James's father, a noted atheist and intellectual, found his atheism confounded by James's revival and saw his years of denying the existence of God wiped out completely, and was never able to write again after that fateful day.

The effect of this discovery is to create a situation in which one must deal with what faith is and how it is to be interpreted. The question at issue in the play is not whether in fact God brought James back to life, but rather how those involved in the event—James, William, and Henry Callifer—must in spite of any evidence or rational explanation understand the event. To a person they interpret it as a miracle, as an affirmation of God's presence, and that affirmation takes on different meaning for each of them and affects each differently. At the opening of the play one is mystified as to why it is so crucial that James be prevented from seeing his dying father. At the end of the play it is revealed that he is a pariah to his father, that his father could not abide his presence because it affirmed to him what he had spent the best years of his life denying: that God exists. For William it is a trap in which his faith is tested but his pride also unmasked; for if he denies the efficacy of his sacrifice, then he denies God, unless he can reach outside the bounds of mere causality and conceive of a God whose mercy and will are infinite and without rational cause. This he cannot do, and the result is that his life is a wasteland.

For James the revelation is in itself a resurrection of himself, for no matter in what way he was snatched from the jaws of death on that day, the "facts" to him are as clear proof as were the wounds to St. Thomas, and, restored to himself, he finally has both a past and a future, where before the revelation he was doomed to exist in a meaningless present. There must be for James a sense of the providential in that event, and he grasps its meaning in terms of himself, as freedom from the ignorance that hung over his life like a cloud. At the close of the play young Anne, who is almost the same age James was at the time of the suicide, affirms it in her dream, in which she dreams that she was going down the path to the potting shed and "there was a lion there fast asleep." This lion does not attack her but instead licks her hand. Like the lion that protects Una and sacrifices his life for her in Book I of Edmund Spenser's *Faerie Queene*, this lion is a sign of God's care, a care that confounds a confirmed atheist, saves a confused young boy, and tests the faith of one of his servants. *The*

Potting Shed has been criticized for its heavy religiosity, but its impact dramatically and its integration of drama and theme make it Greene's most impressive play and one of his major works.

Nonfiction

As a writer of nonfiction prose Greene deserves to be more widely known. His output has been substantial by any standard, so voluminous as to require a much deeper study than this brief survey can hope to be, and he has continued to bring to the tasks of reportage, reviewing, and commentary the same high professional skills evident in his other writing.[8] The body of his work can for convenience be divided into four categories: reportage, occasional essays, literature and film criticism, and autobiography.

Greene is very much in the tradition of the great French essayist and father of the modern essay, Michel de Montaigne, for like Montaigne he adopts, especially in his more personal prose, an almost uncaring stance toward his reader. One is reminded of Montaigne's prefatory comment to his *Essays* in 1588: "I myself am the matter of my book; you would be unreasonable to spend your leisure on so frivolous a subject."[9] Too, like Montaigne, Greene uses his essays as a means of self-discovery (as he has also done with his fiction). He asks Montaigne's eternal question, "Que sais-je?"—What do

I know? True to this spirit Greene provokes, aggravates, but never ceases to try to advance one's awareness of an issue through his efforts to be honest and direct.

Like so many other successful novelists Greene began as a journalist. Though he abandoned journalism in 1930 for a precarious career as a novelist, he returned to it after World War II and, primarily as a free-lancer, provided fine articles on political upheavals in Latin America, especially Haiti and Cuba; on the collapse of French imperialism in Indochina; on the Malay uprisings; and on the Mau Mau rebellion in Kenya.[10] These new stories and longer in-depth pieces are models of careful, balanced, and informed journalism.

Greene's occasional essays are highly individual and convey the image of an intensely private person but one of strong convictions. His preface to Kim Philby's memoir, *My Silent War*, attests to that sense of personal loyalty that has always been a mark of Greene's personal style, as do his many letters to various newspapers on political issues over the years.[11] Perhaps his best essay in this category is his address of 6 June 1969, on receiving the Shakespeare Prize from the University of Hamburg, titled "The Virtue of Disloyalty."[12] It is a highly personal and original expression of Greene's conviction that national allegiances (that is, loyalties) must necessarily be subordinate in any ethic to the loyalty one has to personal allegiances and to personal convictions. It must have struck his listeners as audacious that Greene would single out Shakespeare himself for criticism on that point for his commitment to bourgeois values and a reluctance to embrace disloyalty: "This bourgeois poet on his way to his house in Stratford and his coat of arms . . ." The essay is not only valuable for the light it sheds on novels like *Our Man in Havana* and *The Human Factor* but also because at a time when true patriotism is often confused with patriotic rhetoric, Greene has had the courage to point out the duplicity of such posturing.

Greene's literature and film criticism attests to his wide-ranging mind. His reading has been voluminous and eclectic, and is reflected in the variety of his essays on literary topics. As a critic Greene takes the stance of an educated reader/reviewer rather than a critic or critical theorist in the contemporary sense. His technique is to show himself a skilled reader interested in particular qualities that strike his imagination. The result is a kind of critical writing that does not attempt breadth and coherence but is full of insight, particularly regarding technique, into writers whom Greene himself admires. These include, of course, his favorites, Ford Madox Ford and Henry James; his essays on them are classic, as are his essays on Dickens, Beatrix Potter, and Francis Parkman, among others.

From 1935 to 1940 Greene reviewed films for the *New Statesman and Nation,* at a time when film had yet to be taken seriously as an art form.[13] Greene was fortunate to be in on the early development of this new medium and the first to recognize the artistry and the

SHORT STORIES, PLAYS, ESSAYS

genius of many actors and directors whom film historians and critics have elevated today to the rank of artist. His critical view of American culture, contrary to the opinions of some, allowed him to be all the more valuable as a critic of American film, for it gave him a cultural perspective that seldom can be found in the early days of film criticism except in his judgments. At times his frankness caused him and his publishers considerable grief, as did his famous review for *Night and Day* of Shirley Temple in *Wee Willie Winkie*.[14] In settlement of a lawsuit filed by 20th Century-Fox, Greene and *Night and Day* were required to pay £4,000 in damages. Yet it was precisely this critical honesty that made Greene such a provocative and valued critic. For film historians his reviews are required reading.

Greene's most important work is in the area of autobiography. Included in that category his two best known travel narratives, since they are journeys into Greene's psyche as well as journeys to geographical places. The first, *Journey Without Maps* (1936), has only recently received the attention it deserves. Withdrawn initially from publication because of a threatened libel suit, it has now become a classic, and is perhaps the single most important volume he has written as a window on his character. It was undertaken on assignment from Longmans, Green and covered a journey Greene and his cousin Barbara took in 1934–35 in Liberia. She also wrote and published an account, *Land Benighted* (1938), which provides an interesting point of comparison to Greene's.[15]

UNDERSTANDING GRAHAM GREENE

What is perhaps striking about Greene's is the manner in which he makes his experiences in Liberia resonate against his own childhood years. The result is a fascinating discovery of land and self simultaneously.

The Lawless Roads (1939), Greene's second travel book, led directly to the writing of *The Power and the Glory*. It too came at a time of stress in Greene's life. Unlike *Journey Without Maps* this narrative is not so heavily steeped in his past as it is in his immediate perspective, which is a quality that the best travel literature must have if it is to succeed. Like *Journey Without Maps* it too abounds both in the special revelation Greene brings to his reportage and in the excellent grasp of the particular that allows him to evoke a Mexico in the grip of religious and political turmoil.

Equally fascinating are Greene's two essays "The Lost Childhood" and the "The Revolver in the Corner Cupboard," and his autobiography of his life up to 1932, *A Sort of Life*.[16] The two earlier essays are incorporated into the autobiography, but they also deserve to stand independently as brilliant essays. The whole book presents a fascinating portrait of a troubled but gifted child moving through the early stages of his life. "The Lost Childhood" takes its title from lines from a poem by A. E., quoted by Greene, "In the lost boyhood of Judas /Christ was betrayed," and discusses the shaping qualities of childhood, both the world of childhood experience and the world of childhood reading. "The Revolver in the Corner Cupboard" is a disturbing essay that describes a period in Greene's life when he was suffering from severe depression and had taken to playing russian roulette to cure his boredom. It is a classic piece of confessional literature and sets the tone for much of Greene's later autobiographical sketches.

A Sort of Life (1971) is a fascinating yet perplexing book. Included are the two essays above and material from *Journey Without Maps*. Those necessarily incomplete narratives are expanded and extended. The title itself reveals much—not a life, just a sort of life. Without yielding his privacy in areas that affect his family, Greene fills out in remarkable and enlightening detail his years of growing up, the special agony of being the headmaster's son, those years of torment, then the wasted years at Oxford and the desperate early years of his writing career. It is a window on himself and on England between the wars, and provides a highly discreet but no less revealing view of a most complex writer and person.

Notes

1. Greene himself makes the association between author and character in Marie-Françoise Allain, *The Other Man: Conversations with Graham Greene* (New York: Simon and Schuster, 1983) 122.

2. Gwenn R. Boardman, *Graham Greene: The Aesthetics of Exploration* (Gainesville: University of Florida Press, 1971) 160–69, offers an illuminating explication.

3. *Collected Stories* (London: Bodley Head and Heinemann, 1972) 188.

4. *Ways of Escape* (London: Bodley Head, 1980) 237–45.

5. A helpful overview of Greene's dramatic career and interests is provided by Germaine Goetz, "Greene the Dramatist," *Essays in Graham Greene*, 1 (1987): 127–68.

6. *Collected Plays* (Harmondsworth: Penguin, 1985) 64.

7. *A Sort of Life* (London: Bodley Head, 1971) 86; Allain 149–50.

8. For a list of Greene's pieces see Wobbe, *Graham Greene: A Bibliography* (New York: Garland, 1979) sections B and C. Many of Greene's essays have been gathered into *Collected Essays* (London: Bodley Head, 1969).

9. *Selections from the Essays,* trans. and ed. Donald M. Frame (Arlington Heights, IL: Crofts Classics) 3.

10. "Malaya, the Forgotten War," *Life* 30 July 1951: 51–54; "Kenya as I See It," London *Sunday Times* 27 Sept., 4 Oct. 1953; "A Few Pipes, Extracts from an Indo-China Journal," *London Magazine* Dec. 1954: 17–24; "Return to Cuba," London *Sunday Telegraph* 22 Sept. 1963: 4–5; "Nightmare Republic," London *Sunday Telegraph* 29 Sept. 1963: 4–5.

11. A good selection of them can be found in Maria Couto, *Graham Greene: On the Frontier* (New York: St. Martin's, 1988) 222–29.

12. Printed in *The Portable Graham Greene,* ed. Philip Stratford (Harmondsworth: Penguin, 1977) 606–10.

13. Greene's film reviews are published in *The Pleasure-Dome: The Collected Film Criticism 1935–40* (London: Secker and Warburg, 1972), published in America as *Graham Greene on Film: Collected Film Criticism 1935–40* (New York: Simon and Schuster, 1972).

14. *Ways of Escape* 62–67.

15. Her book has been republished under the title *Too Late to Look Back: Barbara and Graham Greene in Liberia,* intro. by Paul Theroux (London: Bendall, 1981).

16. I do not include here Greene's miscellaneous sequel to this volume, *Ways of Escape,* since it is more a cumulation of introductions to the novels and interspersed autobiographical episodes. While it has much valuable material, it is not quite as focused thematically as is *A Sort of Life.*

BIBLIOGRAPHY

Works by Greene
Books

This list includes both English and American first editions of all books written or edited by Greene and important later editions. Where the Collected Edition volume has been published for a given work, that fact is noted, since the Collected Edition represents Greene's latest intentions as to his text and is an edition for which he read proof and in some cases made substantial revisions. The Collected Edition is published by Heinemann and Bodley Head, and is the most authoritative text produced to date.

The list omits certain scarce limited editions of material published in other books by Greene.

Unless otherwise noted, all works are novels.

Babbling April. Oxford: Basil Blackwell, 1925. (Poems)

The Man Within. London: Heinemann, 1929; Garden City, NY: Doubleday, 1929. Vol. 15 of the Collected Edition, 1976.

The Name of Action. London: Heinemann, 1930; Garden City, NY: Doubleday, 1931.

Rumour at Nightfall. London: Heinemann, 1931; Garden City, NY: Doubleday, 1932.

Stamboul Train. London: Heinemann, 1932. Vol. 12 of the Collected Edition, 1974.

Orient Express. Garden City, NY: Doubleday, 1933. American edition of *Stamboul Train*.

It's a Battlefield. London: Heinemann, 1934; Garden City, NY: Doubleday, 1934. Vol. 2 of the Collected Edition, 1970.

The Old School: Essays by Divers Hands. Ed. Greene. London: Jonathan Cape, 1934.

England Made Me. London: Heinemann, 1935; Garden City, NY: Doubleday, 1935. Vol. 3 of the Collected Edition, 1970. Published as *The Shipwrecked*, 1953.

BIBLIOGRAPHY

The Bear Fell Free. London: Grayson and Grayson, 1935. (Short story, limited edition)

The Basement Room and Other Stories. London: Cresset, 1935.

Journey Without Maps. London: Heinemann, 1936; Garden City, NY: Doubleday, 1936. Vol. 18 of the Collected Edition, 1978. (Travel)

A Gun for Sale. London: Heinemann, 1936. Vol. 9 of the Collected Edition, 1973.

This Gun for Hire. Garden City, NY: Doubleday, 1936. American edition of *A Gun for Sale.*

Brighton Rock. London: Heinemann, 1938; New York: Viking, 1938. Vol. 1 of the Collected Edition, 1970.

The Lawless Roads. London: Heinemann, 1939. Vol. 19 of the Collected Edition, 1978. (Travel)

Another Mexico. New York: Viking, 1939. American edition of *The Lawless Roads.*

The Confidential Agent. London: Heinemann, 1939; New York: Viking, 1939. Vol. 7 of the Collected Edition, 1971.

The Power and the Glory. London: Heinemann, 1940. Vol. 5 of the Collected Edition, 1971.

The Labyrinthine Ways. New York: Viking, 1940. American edition of *The Power and the Glory.*

British Dramatists. London: Collins, 1942. (Criticism)

The Ministry of Fear. London: Heinemann, 1943; New York: Viking, 1943. Vol. 10 of the Collected Edition, 1973.

The Little Train. Norwich: Jarrold and Sons, 1946 (juvenile, published under the name of the illustrator, Dorothy Craigie); New York: Lothrop, 1958 (first publication under Greene's name).

Nineteen Stories. London: Heinemann, 1947; New York: Viking, 1949.

BIBLIOGRAPHY

The Heart of the Matter. London: Heinemann, 1948; New York: Viking, 1948. Vol. 6 of the Collected Edition, 1971.

Why Do I Write? An Exchange of Views between Elizabeth Bowen, Graham Greene, and V. S. Pritchett. London: Percival Marshall, 1948.

The Third Man and The Fallen Idol. London: Heinemann, 1950.

The Third Man. New York: Viking, 1950.

The Third Man. London: Lorrimer, 1968. (Film script)

The Third Man: Loser Takes All. Vol. 16 of the Collected Edition, 1976.

The Little Fire Engine. London: Jarrold and Sons, 1950. Published in America as *The Little Red Fire Engine*. New York: Lothrop, 1953. (Juvenile)

The Best of Saki. Ed. Greene. London: Bodley Head, 1950; New York: Viking, 1961.

The Lost Childhood and Other Essays. London: Eyre and Spottiswoode, 1951; New York: Viking, 1952.

The End of the Affair. London: Heinemann, 1951; New York: Viking, 1951. Vol. 13 of the Collected Edition, 1974.

The Little Horse Bus. London: Jarrold and Sons, 1952; New York: Lothrop, 1954. (Juvenile)

The Shipwrecked. New York: Viking, 1953. Later American edition of *England Made Me*.

The Living Room. London: Heinemann, 1953; New York: Viking, 1954. (Play)

The Little Steamroller. London: Max Parrish, 1953; New York: Lothrop, 1955. (Juvenile)

Nino Caffè. New York: Knoedler, 1953. (Pamphlet)

Essais catholiques. Trans. Marcelle Sibon. Paris: Editions du seuil, 1953.

BIBLIOGRAPHY

Twenty-One Stories. London: Heinemann, 1954; New York: Viking, 1962.

Loser Takes All. London: Heinemann, 1955; New York: Viking, 1957. With *The Third Man*, Vol. 16 of the Collected Edition, 1976.

The Quiet American. London: Heinemann, 1955; New York: Viking, 1956. Vol. 11 of the Collected Edition, 1973.

The Spy's Bedside Book. Ed. Greene and Hugh Greene. London: Rupert Hart-Davis, 1957.

The Potting Shed. London: Heinemann, 1958; New York: Viking, 1957. (Play)

Our Man in Havana. London: Heinemann, 1958; New York: Viking, 1958. Vol. 4 of the Collected Edition, 1970.

The Complaisant Lover. London: Heinemann, 1959; New York: Viking, 1961. (Play)

A Visit to Morin. London: Heinemann, 1960. (Short story, limited edition)

A Burnt-out Case. London: Heinemann, 1961; New York: Viking 1961. Vol. 14 of the Collected Edition, 1974.

In Search of a Character. London: Bodley Head, 1961; New York: Viking, 1962. (Travel)

The Bodley Head Ford Madox Ford. Ed. Greene. 4 vols. London: Bodley Head, 1962–63.

Introductions to Three Novels. Stockholm: P. A. Norstedt & Söners, 1962.

A Sense of Reality. London: Bodley Head, 1963; New York: Viking, 1963. (Short stories)

Carving a Statue. London: Bodley Head, 1964. (Play)

The Comedians. London: Bodley Head, 1966; New York: Viking, 1966. Vol. 17 of the Collected Edition, 1976.

BIBLIOGRAPHY

Victorian Detective Fiction. Ed. Greene and Dorothy Glover. London: Bodley Head, 1966. (Catalog of the Glover-Greene collection, in a limited edition)

May We Borrow Your Husband? And Other Comedies of the Sexual Life. London: Bodley Head, 1967; New York: Viking, 1967. (Short stories)

Collected Essays. London: Bodley Head, 1969; New York: Viking, 1969.

Travels with My Aunt. London: Bodley Head, 1969; New York: Viking, 1970. Vol. 20 of the Collected Edition, 1980.

A Sort of Life. London: Bodley Head, 1971; New York: Simon and Schuster, 1971. (Autobiography)

Collected Stories. London: Bodley Head and Heinemann, 1972; New York: Viking, 1973. Vol. 8 of the Collected Edition, 1972.

The Pleasure-Dome: The Collected Film Criticism 1935–40. London: Secker and Warburg, 1972.

Graham Greene on Film: Collected Film Criticism 1935–40. New York: Simon and Schuster, 1972. American edition of *The Pleasure-Dome*.

The Honorary Consul. London: Bodley Head, 1973; New York: Simon and Schuster, 1973. Vol. 21 of the Collected Edition, 1980.

Lord Rochester's Monkey. London: Bodley Head, 1974; New York: Viking, 1974. (Biography)

An Impossible Woman: The Memories of Dottoressa Moor of Capri. Ed. Greene. London: Bodley Head, 1975; New York: Viking, 1975.

The Return of A. J. Raffles. London: Bodley Head, 1975; New York: Simon and Schuster, 1976. (Play)

BIBLIOGRAPHY

Shades of Greene: The Televised Stories of Graham Greene. London: Heinemann, 1976.

The Human Factor. London: Bodley Head, 1978; New York: Simon and Schuster, 1978. Vol. 22 of the Collected Edition, 1982.

Doctor Fischer of Geneva, or the Bomb Party. London: Bodley Head, 1980; New York: Simon and Schuster, 1980.

Ways of Escape. London: Bodley Head, 1980; New York: Simon and Schuster, 1980. (Autobiography)

The Great Jowett. London: Bodley Head, 1981. (Radio play; limited edition)

Monsignor Quixote. London: Bodley Head, 1982; New York: Simon and Schuster, 1982.

J'Accuse—The Dark Side of Nice. London: Bodley Head, 1982. (Exposé)

A Quick Look Behind: Footnotes to an Autobiography. Los Angeles: Sylvester and Orphanos, 1983. (Poems)

Yes and No: For Whom the Bell Chimes. London: Bodley Head, 1983. (Plays)

Getting to Know the General. London: Bodley Head, 1984; New York: Simon and Schuster, 1984. (Reminiscence)

The Tenth Man. London: Bodley Head and Anthony Blond, 1985; New York: Simon and Schuster, 1985.

Collected Plays. Harmondsworth: Penguin, 1985.

Graham Greene Country. With Paul Hogarth. Preface and commentary by Greene. London: Pavilion and Michael Joseph, 1986.

The Captain and the Enemy. London: Reinhardt, 1988; New York: Viking, 1988.

BIBLIOGRAPHY

Works about Greene
Bibliographies

Cassis, A. F. *Graham Greene: An Annotated Bibliography of Criticism*. Metuchen, NJ: Scarecrow Press, 1981. A highly reliable and thorough bibliography of works about Greene through 1979, with excellent annotations and useful indexes.

Miller, Robert H. *Graham Greene: A Descriptive Catalog*. Lexington: University Press of Kentucky, 1979. Catalog of first editions and other rarities, providing detailed bibliographical information not available elsewhere.

Wobbe, R. A. *Graham Greene: A Bibliography and Guide to Research*. New York: Garland, 1979. The most thorough primary bibliography to date, covering publications and some manuscript materials through 1976. Section on secondary materials is superseded by Cassis.

Books

Adamson, Judith. *Graham Greene and Cinema*. Norman, OK: Pilgrim Books, 1984. Discusses all aspects of Greene's association with the cinema, including his reviewing. The most thorough study to date. (See also Falk and Phillips, below.)

Allain, Marie-Françoise. *The Other Man: Conversations with Graham Greene*. Trans. by Guido Waldeman. New York: Simon and Schuster, 1983. Originally published in French as *L'Autre et son double* (Paris: Belfond, 1981). A most important set of interviews with Greene on wide-ranging issues.

Allott, Kenneth, and Miriam Farris. *The Art of Graham Greene*. New York: Russell and Russell, 1963. One of the earliest critical studies, invaluable for its interpretation of Greene's work from *The Man Within* through *The Heart of the Matter*.

BIBLIOGRAPHY

Bergonzi, Bernard. *Reading the Thirties: Texts and Contexts*. Pittsburgh: University of Pittsburgh Press, 1978. Sees much of Greene's fiction in the context of the decade as conservative in its basic impulses. Provocative and helpful readings.

Boardman, Gwenn R. *Graham Greene: The Aesthetics of Exploration*. Gainesville: University of Florida Press, 1971. Valuable study of the relationship between landscape and fiction, of the metaphor of exploration as it relates to Greene's development as an artist.

Couto, Maria. *Graham Greene: On the Frontier*. New York: St. Martin's, 1988. The most useful study to date of the political dimensions of Greene's fiction.

Davis, Elizabeth. *Graham Greene: The Artist as Critic*. Fredericton, NB, Can.: York Press, 1984. Discusses Greene's nonfiction writings, tracing especially his developing views on the art of fiction and the creative process.

DeVitis, A. A. *Graham Greene*. Rev. ed. Boston: Twayne, 1986. An excellent all-round introductory book on Greene stressing religious themes.

Evans, Robert O., ed. *Graham Greene: Some Critical Considerations*. Lexington: University of Kentucky Press, 1967. Collection of articles on Greene's fiction with emphasis on religious fiction.

Falk, Quentin. *Travels in Greeneland: The Cinema of Graham Greene*. London: Quartet Books, 1984. A helpful survey of Greene's cinematic works. (See also Adamson, above, and Phillips, below.)

Hynes, Samuel, ed. *Graham Greene: A Collection of Critical Essays*. Englewood Cliffs, NJ: Prentice-Hall, 1973. Important collection of major articles on Greene stressing religious fiction.

BIBLIOGRAPHY

Lodge, David. *Graham Greene*. Columbia Essays on Modern Writers Series 17. New York: Columbia University Press, 1971. An excellent discussion of technique in the novels, with an especially compelling analysis of *The End of the Affair*.

Madaule, Jacques. *Graham Greene*. Paris: Editions du temps, 1949. Discusses familiar themes in Greene's fiction, particularly religious, from early work through *The Heart of the Matter*.

Mesnet, Marie-Béatrice. *Graham Greene and the Heart of the Matter: An Essay*. London: Cresset, 1954. A study of the three major religious novels—*Brighton Rock*, *The Power and the Glory*, and *The Heart of the Matter*—with a strongly theocentric interpretation.

Phillips, Gene D. *Graham Greene: The Films of His Fiction*. New York: Teachers College Press, 1974. Discusses Greene's own film scripts of his work and those of others. (See also Adamson and Falk, above.)

Radell, Karen. *Affirmation in a Moral Wasteland: Ford Madox Ford and Graham Greene*. New York: Peter Lang, 1987. Helpful analysis of the relation between Greene and Ford, with useful comparisons of Greene and T. S. Eliot.

Sharrock, Roger. *Saints, Sinners, and Comedians: The Novels of Graham Greene*. Notre Dame, IN: University of Notre Dame Press, 1984. Extremely valuable analysis of the range of Greene's fiction with emphasis on more recent schools of interpretation.

Sherry, Norman. *The Life of Graham Greene*. Vol. I. London: Jonathan Cape, 1989; New York: Viking, 1989. The first volume of what is to be the most exhaustive biographical treatment of Greene to date, covering the years from his birth to the opening of World War II.

BIBLIOGRAPHY

Stratford, Philip. *Faith and Fiction: Creative Process in Greene and Mauriac*. Notre Dame, IN: University of Notre Dame Press, 1964. Comparison of Greene and his contemporary, the French writer François Mauriac. Excellent analysis of a major religious fiction.

Thomas, Brian. *An Underground Fate: The Idiom of Romance in the Later Novels of Graham Greene*. Athens: University of Georgia Press, 1988. Argues that the prevailing form of Greene's fiction from 1950 onward is that of romance.

Wolfe, Peter. *Graham Greene: The Entertainer*. Carbondale: Southern Illinois University Press, 1972. Covers the "entertainments" of Greene's early career.

Articles

Allen, Walter. "Graham Greene." *Writers of To-day*. Ed. Denys Val Baker. London: Sidgwick and Jackson, 1946. 15–28. Discusses the novels and their relation to theological dogma and heresies.

Burgess, Anthony. "The Greene and the Red: Politics in the Novels of Graham Greene." *Urgent Copy: Literary Studies*. London: Jonathan Cape, 1968. 13–20.

Cheney, Lynne. "Joseph Conrad's *The Secret Agent* and Graham Greene's *It's a Battlefield:* A Study in Structural Meanings." *Modern Fiction Studies* 16 (Spring 1970): 117–31.

Essays in Graham Greene: An Annual. Ed. Peter Wolfe. Greenwood, FL: Penkevill Publishing, 1987–. Several important articles on the novels and plays.

Evans, Robert O. "The Satanist Fallacy of *Brighton Rock*." *Graham Greene: Some Critical Considerations*, ed. Evans. Lexington: University of Kentucky Press, 1967. Argues against a heroic interpretation of Pinkie, vis à vis Satanist arguments of critics of *Paradise Lost*.

BIBLIOGRAPHY

Higdon, David Leon. "Betrayed Intentions: The Text of Graham Greene's *The End of the Affair*." *Library* n.s. 6, 1 (1979): 70–77.
———. "Graham Greene's Second Thoughts: The Text of *The Heart of the Matter*." *Studies in Bibliography* 30 (1977): 249–56. (See also Stratford, below.)
———. "Saint Catherine, von Hügel, and Graham Greene's *The End of the Affair*." *English Studies* 62 (1982): 46–52. Traces the sources of the novel.
Hynes, Joseph. "The 'Facts' at *The Heart of the Matter*." *Texas Studies in Literature and Language* 13 (1972): 711–26. Provides an excellent insight into the nature of Scobie.
Kermode, Frank. "Mr. Greene's Eggs and Crosses." *Graham Greene: A Collection of Critical Essays*, ed. Samuel Hynes. Englewood Cliffs, NJ: Prentice-Hall, 1973. 126–37. Controversial but provocative look at *A Burnt-out Case*.
Lewis, R. W. B. "The Trilogy." *Graham Greene: A Collection of Critical Essays*, ed. Samuel Hynes. Englewood Cliffs, NJ: Prentice-Hall, 1973. 49–74 An excellent analysis of the major religious novels: *Brighton Rock*, *The Power and the Glory*, and *The Heart of the Matter*.
Marion, Denis. "Graham Greene." *Le table ronde* Feb. 1950: 173–79. A dark but impressive interpretation of the pessimistic aspects of Greene's view of the world.
Masters, Anthony. "Graham Greene: The Abrasive Spy." *Literary Agents: The Novelist as Spy*. Oxford: Blackwell, 1987. 114–33. A fairly detailed narrative of Greene's service in MI6, drawing heavily on Greene's own accounts, with passing comments on some of the spy novels.
Modern Fiction Studies 3 (1957). Entire issue devoted to various aspects of Greene's work.

BIBLIOGRAPHY

O'Faolain, Sean. "Graham Greene: I Suffer; Therefore I Am." *The Vanishing Hero.* London: Eyre and Spottiswoode, 1956. 73–79. Argues that Greene's characters lose force in being subordinated to the overriding theme of evil.

Orwell, George. "The Sanctified Sinner." *Graham Greene: A Collection of Critical Essays,* ed. Samuel Hynes. Englewood Cliffs, NJ: Prentice-Hall, 1973. 105–09. A highly critical view of *The Heart of the Matter.*

Shuttleworth, Martin, and Simon Raven. "The Art of Fiction III: Graham Greene." *Paris Review* 1 (Autumn 1953): 24–41. Interview with Greene on his fiction, stressing ideas and techniques.

Stratford, Philip. "Second Thoughts on Graham Greene's 'Second Thoughts': The Five Texts of *The Heart of the Matter.*" *Studies in Bibliography* 31 (1978): 263–66. Corrects Higdon's article cited above.

Traversi, Derek. "Graham Greene." *Twentieth Century* 149 (1951): 231–40. Traces development of themes from *Brighton Rock* to *The Heart of the Matter.*

Walker, Ronald G. "World without End: An Approach to Narrative Structure in Greene's *The End of the Affair.*" *English Studies* 26 (1984): 218–41. A careful and ingenious analysis of the complex structure of this complex novel.

Wright, David G. "Greene's *Brighton Rock.*" *Explicator* 41 (Summer 1983): 52–53. Examines the meaning of Greene's title and the significance of Brighton rock as a symbol.

Zabel, Morton Dauwen. "Graham Greene: The Best and the Worst." *Craft and Character in Modern Fiction.* New York: Viking, 1957. Sharply critical and acute exploration of the achievements and failings of Greene's work.

INDEX

Page numbers in bold type indicate extended discussions of Greene's works.

INDEX

INDEX

INDEX

INDEX

INDEX